Concentration Camps
A Traveler's Guide
to World War II Sites

Marc Terrance

About the Author

Marc Terrance has traveled extensively to the major concentration camps & holocaust sites of Europe over the past 20 years.

He is not Jewish. Ever since he was a child he has been drawn to the subject of the Holocaust. After watching hours of the old black and white archival films on television, he felt compelled to start visiting these sites to learn more. It was during these trips that he found it very difficult to find exact directions, so in 1998 he decided to put all of his findings into a book, so that anyone who wishes to visit these places will be able to find them easily. Having already visited many of these camps over the years, his next mission was to re-visit ALL of the major Holocaust sites in one research trip.

By himself, in the fall of 1998, Marc spent 155 Hours on Trains making over 80 Connections through 6 Countries to visit 39 Sites in 25 Days! (and they said it couldn't be done!). In most cases he walked from the nearest train station to the camps, hand-drawing maps, jotting down landmarks and street names and gathering information from every source. It was an exhausting experience, both physically and mentally, but one of the most rewarding journeys of his life. He plans to continue his studies and perhaps add more sites to this book for future editions.

ISBN: 1-58112-839-8

Universal Publishers/UPUBLISH.COM
2003

www.upublish.com/books/terrance.htm

www.ConcentrationCampGuide.com

ACKNOWLEDGMENTS

Thanks to:

Rudi Haunschmied, Martha Gammer and Siegi Witzany-Durda for their help in Austria and for their tireless work to keep the memory of Gusen camp alive.

Dr. Lucja Pawlicka-Nowak, Zdzislaw Lorek and Izabela Lorek for their kindness and help while I was visiting Chelmno camp in Poland.

Slawek Nowodworski for his guidance in Poland at the camps of Sobibór and Belzec.

Gaby Oelrichs of the House of the Wannsee Conference in Berlin for her help and encouragement.

Sherrie & Karl Meyers, Jim Bauman and Marty Billdt for their technical expertise in helping set up the formatting of this book.

Leslie Fawns, Teresa Hennessy, Rhonda Acosta, Emily Holley and David Mullett for their help with editing and proofreading.

To Kip for his incredible patience, understanding & help on this project.

And sincere thanks to the many wonderful people who work at the camps and museums for sending me the information I needed to make the journey and do the research for this book.

NOTE:
If you can only go to ONE Camp and can make the trip, I'd Suggest AUSCHWITZ. If you have never been to one of these memorials, be prepared. Of all the camps I've visited, this is the most horrendous, most vivid and exhausting to experience. I truly believe everyone NEEDS to see this, to experience what people can do to other human beings, and to learn from it so that it will never happen again.

Most of the camps have Free Admission.
Some are Closed on Mondays.

Wherever Prices or Time Schedules are shown, please use them only as a point of reference as they are Subject to Change.

CONTENTS

INTRODUCTION

During World War II the Nazi Government under Adolf Hitler perpetrated one of the most horrendous chapters in human history. There have been other crimes against humanity in other places and other times, but what happened in Europe from the early 1930's-1945 became known as the HOLOCAUST and showed "Mans Inhumanity to Man" in its many acts of cruelty, torture, imprisonment and murder. So that we may never forget, many of the Concentration Camps and other associated sites have been preserved as memorials.

I have visited many of these places over the years and decided to put my impressions into a book along with important information for Travelers. The purpose of this book is to guide those who wish to make these journeys.

These sites are not fun tourist theme parks, they are serious historical memorials dedicated to the memory of those who perished. Years ago when I first started traveling to the camps, I sometimes would find myself alone except for a handful of other visitors. Now, after a renewed interest in the Holocaust with movies like "Schindler's List" etc, many many people are visiting these sites. In some cases you will come across rows of tour buses, school children on field trips and large groups of tourists toting cameras and video equipment.

I try to think of this as a good thing as long as people respect what they are seeing and act accordingly. Too often youngsters can be seen in groups laughing and joking. They obviously have not been prepared beforehand about what it is they are witnessing.

It is important that we visit these sites and tell others about our experiences to help keep the memory alive. I HIGHLY recommend that anyone making these journeys study, read, see films and THINK about the Holocaust BEFORE going. What you will experience can change your life and your understanding of the Holocaust.

Hatred, bigotry and intolerance have been prevalent throughout history. When we cannot accept others who are different than ourselves, be it Race, Religion, Sexual Orientation or Ethnic Background, that's where the trouble begins.

We are all human beings and we all need to learn to celebrate our differences and live in peace. When you visit these memorials realize that all it took was the hatred of a few high ranking individuals to ignite the fear and anger in thousands of people. This led normally intelligent citizens to either go along with or turn their heads and ignore one of histories most brutal times.

We cannot afford to let the ignorance or intolerance of any group today or in the future, lead our citizens down the road to ruin by trying to discriminate against ANYONE.

The Nazis set up camps all over Europe. Although the most infamous of those, Auschwitz & Dachau received the most notoriety, there were hundreds of other camps & sub-camps.

Most of the "Death Camps" were set up in the East, in Poland. But the crimes against humanity were carried out in all of these places. Even Today, it comes as a shock to some people that not all those who were persecuted under the Nazis were Jewish.

It is true, make no mistake about it, that the majority of those who suffered, were, indeed Jewish, but the Nazis also targeted a great many others in their plan to annihilate those whom they considered inferior and not part of the perfect Aryan race. Gypsies, Jehovah's Witnesses, Gay people, just to name a few. Resistance Fighters or anyone caught helping the Jews or those fleeing for their lives were also arrested and sent to prison camps where many of them also died from being over-worked or starved or murdered.

The mentally ill, retarded, dimwitted & alcoholics were also targeted and referred to as "Useless Eaters". These people were sent to institutions that from the outside appeared to be hospitals, but inside, these poor unfortunates, many of them non-Jews, were gassed all in the name of making the Perfect German Aryan Race. Let the visions you will see during your travels open your eyes to what can happen and open your hearts to your fellow man.

I dedicate this book to the millions who perished.
To all those who make the journey to see these sites,
I say, spread these words – NEVER AGAIN!

Recommended Viewing: **Memory of the Camps**
Frontline – TV Broadcast
www.pbs.org/wgbh/pages/frontline/camp/

Recommended Reading: **Historical Atlas**
of the Holocaust
United States Holocaust
Memorial Museum
1996 Macmillan Publishing,
Simon & Schuster

According to regulation No 10
of the Ministry of Education
dated March 6, 1963, children
under the age of 13 are not
allowed in museums of
Martyrdom in Poland.
(Those I asked, said this is
Not strictly enforced).

Look for these symbols
leading to
Concentration Camps in Poland

POLAND

Auschwitz-Birkenau (Oswiecim-Brzezinka)

Address: Panstwowe Muzeum Oswiecim-Brzezinka
ul. Wiezniow Oswiecimia 20
32-620 Oswiecim, Poland

Phone: 48 + 33 + 843 20 22
Fax: 48 + 33 + 843 19 34

E-mail: muzeum@auschwitz.org.pl
Website(s):   www.auschwitz-muzeum.oswiecim.pl
www.spectacle.org/695/ausch.html

Hours: Open **DAILY**
8:00am-3:00pm   December 16 thru end of February
8:00am-4:00pm   March 1 to March 31 &
                November 1 to December 15
8:00am-5:00pm   April 1 to April 30 and
                October 1 to October 31
8:00am-6:00pm   May 1 to May 31 and
                September 1 to September 30
8:00am-7:00pm   June 1 to August 31
CLOSED: January 1, December 25, Easter Sunday

Entrance: Free

9

Schedule:	Plan on spending most of the day to see both parts of this sight: Auschwitz Main Camp & Birkenau. At the very Least you need 4 hours.

Location:	Southern Poland near Krakow

Approx Train Travel Time to Krakow (Glowny Station):

From:	Berlin	10:07
	Lublin	4:25
	Vienna (Wien)	9:05
	Prague (Praha)	12:54
	Auschwitz (Oswiecim)	1:25

By Train:	I've always traveled from Berlin to Krakow Poland and then on to the camp. There are overnight trains from Berlin & Vienna (Wien) that arrive in Krakow around 6am.

Auschwitz is approximately 54 km (33 miles) west of Krakow and is easily reached by train in about 1 hour & 25 minutes.

From Krakow Glowny Station (Main Station) there are several trains daily. Get a train ticket to OSWIECIM (pronounced *OWS VEE ENCH EM*)
(Auschwitz is the German spelling)

Since you will find that English is not readily understood in Poland, unlike most other Western European Countries where it's usually not a problem, it will be helpful to be able to say OSWIECIM when getting your ticket.

Baggage:	Krakow Glowny station has Baggage Lockers, or inside the station there is a Baggage Check Window where you can store your bags if you are only staying the day for sightseeing.

There is a Baggage window outside, but that is not open. Go INSIDE the station.

Baggage storage in most Polish stations is marked
"Przechowalnia Bagazu"
If nobody is attending the counter,
RING THE BELL and they will come out.

NOTE:
Upon arrival at Oswiecim Be sure to time your stay accordingly:

CHECK YOUR RETURN TRAIN SCHEDULE when you ARRIVE in the Morning. Otherwise you might end up taking a Taxi back to Krakow! Trains Back to Krakow Glowny are **NOT** hourly.

There are 2 parts to Auschwitz:
Auschwitz Main Camp & Birkenau. I highly suggest going to the Main Camp first and then Birkenau on the way back & therefore the following directions reflect that route.
This will give you a better perspective on what you are seeing.

By Bus: Stops in front of the train station. Times Posted.

To Walk: <u>20 Minutes to Auschwitz Main Camp</u>.
Walk out the Front of Oswiecim station, you will be on **ul.Powstancow**. Cross the street and turn right. After a short distance the name of the street changes to **Wyzwolenia**.
Auschwitz is on the same street as the train station (it just changes names)
When you come to a Round-a-Bout you will keep to the left (there is a sign over on the right side of the street. Here the street name changes to **ul.Stanislawy Leszcynskiej**
The camp is about 10 minutes walk from this point. As you walk along you will notice a street that veers off to the right and curves up and over a bridge. That is the way to Birkenau which you will be taking on the way back. It is NOT marked on signs that you can see walking in this direction, but as you pass that street and turn around, you will notice a small sign on the side you are walking down directing you there. It can only be seen coming from the other way. (I think they want to be SURE people visit the Main Camp first because there used to be signs in both directions)

11

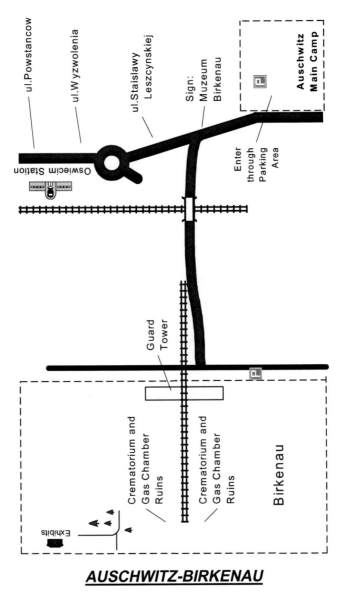

AUSCHWITZ-BIRKENAU

You will come up to the camp on the Left side of the street.

You'll first walk through the parking area (most likely past a lot of tour buses). Then you'll see the large brick buildings that make up most of Auschwitz Main camp.   (main entrance Below)

What Remains:
There is much to see at this site, more so than any other camp.
There is a 15 minute movie (small fee). Buy tickets & check times for the language of choice at window in the entrance hall.

It will take you several hours to walk through and see all the buildings, past barbed wire fences and the familiar Nazi lie over the gate entrance:

ARBEIT MACHT FREI
(Work Makes Freedom)

As you walk down each row of "Blocks" and through each building, you will be shown many different countries memorials to those killed. Be sure to go through each building that is open to the public if you can, as each one is filled with pictures and exhibits.

One has a room full of Human Hair shaved from prisoners heads.
One has a room full of Crutches and Wooden Legs
One has a room full of Shoes, Suitcases, Eyeglasses etc.

There is the original small gas chamber in the basement of one building **(Block 11)**
It was here in the cellar of Block 11 on September 3, 1941 that they carried out the first attempt of mass extermination with gas (Zyclon B) In the yard next to Block 11 is the **"Wall of Death"** where at least 20,000 prisoners were executed by shooting.

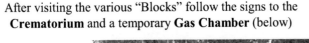
After visiting the various "Blocks" follow the signs to the **Crematorium** and a temporary **Gas Chamber** (below)

You will walk into a huge cement room that was once the mortuary, then converted into a gas chamber. Hundreds could be gassed at a time. Exit into a room where the crematorium ovens are located. Many visitors put flowers and light candles in remembrance.

There are gift shops if you want to purchase videos or picture books. There is also a small cafeteria on the premises.

After visiting Auschwitz main camp, you should then go to Birkenau (3km – 2 miles) which is a 25 minute walk, or from April 15 to October 31 they have a **Bus** that goes between Auschwitz & Birkenau (small fee) It leaves hourly from 10:30am-4:30pm from outside the Cafeteria entrance facing the parking area.

To Walk:
25 Minutes to Birkenau.
Leave Auschwitz the way you came in and walk back toward the train station, but cross the street and walk down the left side now. When you get to that side street marked Muzeum Birkenau (Brzezinka) which goes slightly uphill and over

a small bridge, make a left and walk toward Birkenau about 15 minutes. You will soon see the familiar Watch Tower seen on TV and in movies.

This is where the trains came into the camp for the "Selections".

Birkenau is HUGE! As far as the eye can see are row after row of smoke stacks on foundations which used to be buildings for prisoners. You can walk upstairs in the front Tower Building and look out the windows (good for pictures and to see the vastness of the place)

Walk in to the camp and turn right and go into the first few buildings that are remaining. (see below)

Some show the bunks where people were crammed together to sleep. One building has long rows of holes in cement, (these were the toilets) Imagine, thousands of people rushing in there. They only had a few minutes, no privacy, no toilet paper.

Walk back to the middle and continue down the tracks or path and try to imagine what it was like as the trains pulled in, and people like Dr. Josef Mengele pointed to the left or right and sentenced prisoners to work or be gassed at his whim.

Straight ahead at the very end are the remains of the crematorium and gas chambers. It is a mess of rubble. You can walk down stairs into one of the undressing areas that lead into the gas chambers (no roof)

The Nazis destroyed all this as Soviet troops approached to try and hide what they were doing.

16

If you continue down a small path to your right and through the woods you will see huge tanks. (The Nazis tried to make gasoline with human excrement in these tanks). Continue and you'll come across another building used to store articles stolen from prisoners, and delousing rooms. There are some exhibits (opened in April 2001) in this building. Further on, more crematorium ruins one of which was blown up by the prisoners themselves during a revolt. (they were executed for this)

Because of the sheer SIZE of Birkenau, you can spend several hours wandering, walking and just soaking it all in. As I recommended earlier, go to Auschwitz MAIN Camp first. The pictures, exhibits & dioramas shown in the extensive exhibits there will help you to better visualize what these ruins looked like when they were in operation.

When finished, you can walk back to the train station in about 20 minutes or take the bus back to the Main Camp and walk from there. It's about the same walking distance either way.

Camp Opened: 1940
Date Liberated: January 27, 1945 by the Red Army

Background:
Auschwitz is the most infamous of all the concentration camps mainly because of all the killing centers the Nazis set up, the largest number of deaths occurred here.

Oskar Schindler's Factory:

Address: ul. Lipowa 4   (Lipowa Street)
Krakow, Poland

E-mail: None Available
Website: www.geocities.com/Pentagon/7087/uk009.htm

Hours: This is NOT a museum and is NOT open to the public. It is currently an electronic parts manufacturing plant. Walk by, take a picture if you wish, but there is nothing more to see here.

This is where Oskar Schindler (Schindler's List) had his enamel factory. The Jewish prisoners stayed at nearby Plaszow Concentration Camp and worked here.

Today, a plaque on the factory grounds says in broken English:

*"The Workplace over 1000 Jewish
Nationality Persons. During Second
World War - Saved their life by
Oskar Schindler"*

To Walk:	**5 Minutes.** From Krakow Glowny take the train in the direction of Wieliczka. The first stop (4 minutes from Glowny) is Krakow Zablocie train platform (*not well marked*, just be aware it's the First stop, 4 minutes out). Exit the train and walk Left down the platform to the stairs down to street level. Turn Left and walk through the tunnel under the tracks and down a small path to the street straight ahead. This is ul.Lipowa (Lipowa Street). Halfway down on the Left side is #4

**Recommended
Reading:** Schindler's List
by Thomas Keneally

**Recommended
Viewing:** Schindler's List (1993) B/W 3 hrs. 17 min.
Steven Spielberg – Director
Liam Neeson as Oskar Schindler
Available on Video. MCA Universal Pictures

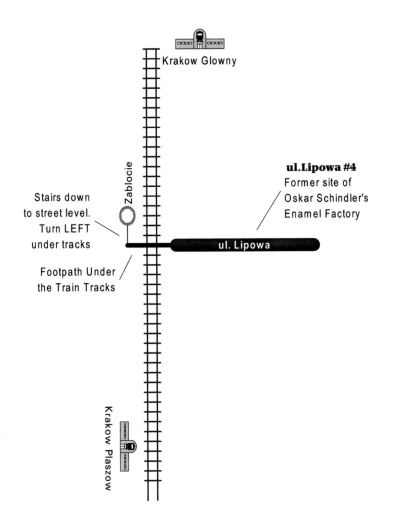

Krakow Glowny

Zablocie

Stairs down
to street level.
Turn LEFT
under tracks

Footpath Under
the Train Tracks

ul.Lipowa #4
Former site of
Oskar Schindler's
Enamel Factory

ul. Lipowa

Krakow Plaszow

SCHINDLER'S FACTORY

Plaszow

Address: Located in a Field. SEE MAP

Hours: There is No Museum, just a couple of monuments, so you may visit at ANY time

Website(s):
www.jewishgen.org/ForgottenCamps/Camps/MainCampsEng.html
www.scrapbookpages.com/Poland/Plaszow/Plaszow01.html

Schedule: Plan on about a half hour to walk around the paths finding the monuments and taking a few pictures.

Approx Train Travel Time to : Krakow Plaszow

From:

Lublin	6:30
Krakow (Zablocie)	0:02 minutes
Krakow (Glowny)	0:05 minutes
Warsaw (Warszawa)	3:00

To Walk: <u>**15 Minutes.**</u> Plaszow station is 2 minutes further down the same line after Zablocie station where Schindler's Factory was.
From Krakow Plaszow station exit the front of the train station, the camp site is about a half mile straight ahead down **ul.Dworcowa**.
The first major intersection is **ul.Wielicka**.
Across the street on the left is a McDonald's!
Cross over ul.Wielicka and continue straight ahead walking slightly uphill up a footpath to **ul.Heltmana** .
Turn right, the street becomes **ul.Jerozolimska**.

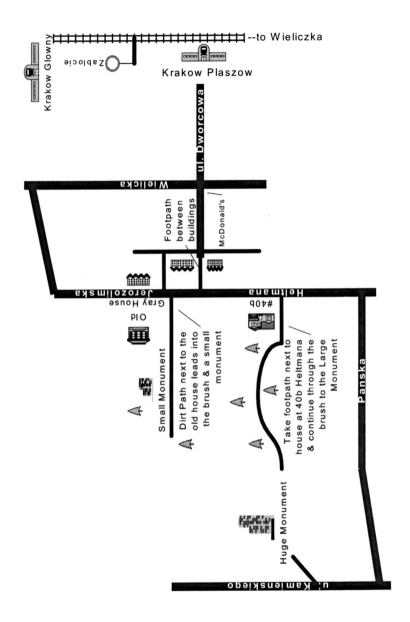

PLASZOW

22

There is a big gray house a few steps down **ul.Jerozolimska** on the Left side of the street.
This house was used as the Plaszow Commandant Amon Goeth's home in the film Schindler's list. His actual house is nearby on the same street.

Take a left down the trail next to the driveway on the left side of this house.

A few steps into the brush area is a very small monument on the Right side of the path.

Litter and garbage is cluttered around.

As a Memorial
It's a Disgrace.

You can continue along this path to find your way to the larger monument or walk back the way you came and continue down Heltmana (see Map)

When you get to the house marked **40b** on the Right side of Heltmana, turn Right. Walk ahead and you will see another dirt path that runs behind the house and into the brush

Follow this path for about 5 minutes and you will come to a HUGE monument.
It faces **ul.H.Kamienskiego** which is a main street, but taking the path is faster to reach the monument.

Walk around the FRONT of the monument. **It's Very Dramatic.**

23

**A huge monument at the former site of the
Plaszow Concentration Camp in Krakow, Poland**

By Bus/Tram: From the City Center: Bus #'s 124, 164, 173
or Tram #'s 3, 43

> **NOTE:** Of all the camp memorials I've been to, this is one of the most neglected and hard to find sites. There are NO signs or markers leading the way to the monuments and there is garbage, broken bottles. and graffiti.

Camp Opened: October 1942

Date Liberated: January 15, 1945 by the Soviets

What Remains:

Absolutely Nothing remains of this camp (depicted in the 1993 movie SCHINDLER'S LIST) but a large hill and field and the Monuments mentioned above. If you saw the movie, you'll remember Kommandant Amon Goeth (pronounced Gert, and portrayed by actor Ralph Fiennes) would shoot prisoners from his balcony. This is the site of the camp that he ran. Many of Oskar Schindler's Jews lived in this camp and worked in his factory during the day. At the end of the war, Goeth was arrested & hanged by the Poles at Plaszow on Sept. 13, 1945.

Stutthof (Sztutowo)

Address: Panstwowe Muzeum Stutthof
ul. Muzealna 6
82-110 Sztutowo, Poland

Phone: 48 + 55 + 247 83 53
Fax: 48 + 55 + 247 83 58

E-mail: Stutthof@softel.com.pl
Website(s):
www.stutthof.pl
www.jewishgen.org/ForgottenCamps/Camps/StutthofEng.html

Hours: Open DAILY
(No Cinema or Guide Service on Mondays)
May 1st thru September 30th 8am-6pm
October 1st thru April 30th 8am-3pm

Entrance: Free

Schedule: Plan on about 2 Hours to see this site.

Location: Northern Poland along the Baltic Coast. 36km –22 mi east of Gdansk (Danzig) at the mouth of the Vistula River.

Approx Train Travel Time to Gdansk Glowny:
From: Berlin   9:25
Krakow   9:40
Warsaw (Warszawa)   4:16
Lublin   6:55

By Bus: **70 Minutes** From Gdansk Glowny (main train station) you need to find the Bus Station.
You do NOT want the buses located out front of the Train Station. These are city buses.

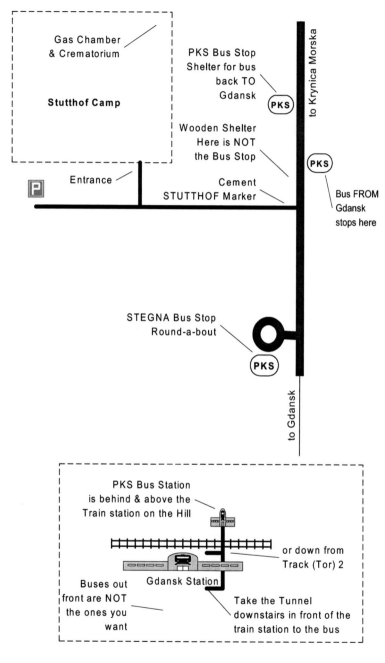

Gas Chamber & Crematorium

Stutthof Camp

Entrance

PKS Bus Stop Shelter for bus back TO Gdansk

PKS

Wooden Shelter Here is NOT the Bus Stop

Cement STUTTHOF Marker

PKS

Bus FROM Gdansk stops here

to Krynica Morska

STEGNA Bus Stop Round-a-bout

PKS

to Gdansk

PKS Bus Station is behind & above the Train station on the Hill

or down from Track (Tor) 2

Buses out front are NOT the ones you want

Gdansk Station

Take the Tunnel downstairs in front of the train station to the bus

STUTTHOF

27

To reach the Bus Station (**PKS**):
Either at the end of Platform (Peron) 2, go downstairs
and turn Left through the tunnel.
OR, go out the Front of the Train station and go
down the stairs to the Left into the tunnel.
Walk to the end of the tunnel and up the Escalators.
The Bus Station is located up on the hill Behind the
train station.

Look for **"Dworzec PKS Autobusowy"**
(PKS denotes Buses in Poland, PKP denotes trains)

You want a Roundtrip ticket to Sztutowo (Stutthof)
You CAN pay the Driver, they make change, but I
suggest buying your ticket in advance at the station.
The bus will be going in the direction of Krynica
Morska. Here is a sample bus schedule:

Gdansk to Sztutowo: 7:20, 9:30, 11:00, 14:00, 15:45
Sztutowo to Gdansk: 11:22, 12:57, 15:11, 16:57, 18:57

As always, write down your destination to show
the ticket agent AND the driver. They most likely
will not understand a word of English.
The bus stop for this route is upstairs to the Right of
the ticket windows
(look for **"wyjscie na stanowiska – 8,9"**)

Sit on the Left side of the bus if you can to see the
signs for the camp. I only noticed 2 along the way, so
keep an eye open. The bus takes about 70 minutes to
reach the camp. When you reach **"Stegna"** where the
bus pulls into a round-a-bout and drops off passen-
gers, the stop for the camp will be coming up soon.

They do NOT announce the stops!

About 2 minutes after it leaves that round-a-bout be looking for a Cement Marker "STUTTHOF" on the Left and a small sign on the Right. If you don't stand up and move for the door, they keep going.

DON'T PANIC when the driver doesn't stop in front of the camp. The Sztutowo Bus Stop is about 100 yards further down the street so you have a moment to jump up and get to the door before the actual stop comes up.

(They will NOT stop at the Camp Entrance)

(See Bus on the Road...*that* is where they drop you off)

It's about a 5 minute walk from the road to the camp gate.

When returning, the bus stop you need to be at is down the road to the Left of the entrance to the camp. (You will see an old wooden structure that looks like a bus stop near the Cement marker. It says Muzeum Stutthof on it, this is NOT the bus stop to Gdansk)
The wooden bus stop you want is further down on the Left
(PAST the stop where you arrived)

Returning you want the bus that says **"Krynica Morska-Gdansk"**
Have **"Gdansk Dworcu Glownym"** (Gdansk Main Train Station) written down to show the driver if you are not sure.

What Remains:
Main Gate, several buildings with exhibits (in Polish Only),
a small gas chamber, crematorium, box car that carried prisoners to this
camp, foundations of Blocks (barracks), monuments and a cinema.

Stutthof Gate

Gas Chamber

Camp Opened: September 2, 1939
Date Liberated: May 9, 1945 by the Soviet Army

Warszawa Ghetto (Warsaw)

Website:
www.scrapbookpages.com/Poland/WarsawGhetto/WarsawGhetto01.html

Schedule: Plan on about an hour to walk around this area. But again, there isn't much to see. You need to do a lot of visualizing.

To Walk: **40 Minutes** From Warszawa (pronounced *Var sha va*) Centralna (Warsaw Main Train Station) exit the station on to Al.Jerozolimskie and turn Left. The next major intersection is Marszalkowska, turn Left. Continue for quite a while passing at least 3 major intersections until you cross Al.Solidarnosci. The name of the street then changes to Gen.Wladyslawa Andersa. A few blocks down turn Left on Nowolipki, then Right on L.Zamenhofa.

A few blocks down you will see a park like area on the Left with the Memorial to the Heroes of the Warsaw Ghetto monument.

Recommend: I suggest taking a city tour that includes this area or hiring a guide for a few hours.

What Remains:

There are several monuments. Pawiak Prison on ul.Dzielna 24/26 has a small exhibit room. Most of the area is now either residential or commercial. Part of this area was walled in during the war to confine the Jews. Now it looks just like any other part of the city.

Memorial to the Heroes of the Warsaw Ghetto on L.Zamenhofa.

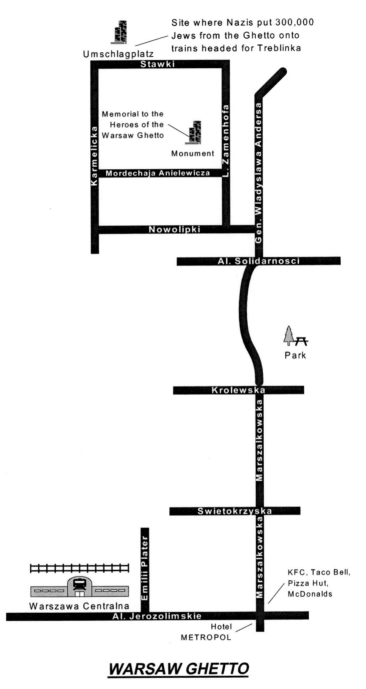

WARSAW GHETTO

Treblinka

Address: For Information Only, NOT the address of the site
Gedenkstätte Treblinki
08-330 Kosow Lacki
Poland

Phone: 48+ 417 – 87 90 76
Fax: 48+ 25 – 242/24

E-mail: None Available
Website(s):   www.deathcamps.org
www.scrapbookpages.com/Poland/Treblinka/index.html

Hours: Open DAILY 9am until Dusk

Entrance: Free

Schedule: Plan on about 30 minutes unless you want to walk
down the path through the woods.

Approx Train Travel Time to Warsaw
(Warszawa Centralna Station):
From: Berlin   8:33
Gdansk   4:16
Krakow (Glowny)   4:40
Lublin   2:16
Moscow   24:25

By Train: 1 Hour. From Warszawa (Warsaw) Centralna station
take a train to Malkinia (pronounced Mal Keen ya).
Then by Taxi (recommended), or Bus to the camp.

Bus from Malkinia: **40 Minutes.**
Bus Schedule: Malkinia-Treblinka 8:55am
(The only buses BACK are at 3:15 & 18:25.
If you get the morning bus TO the camp, you will be
stuck there for HOURS waiting, or walking back
(1 hr & 40 minutes)

Exit the train and walk to the bus stop marked **PKS**, (buses in Poland) located in the parking area between the station and the snack bar.

It's best to buy a bus ticket in the train station. Go inside the front of the station and through the waiting room to the Right into another little room. Buy your ticket from the window marked **"Kasa Biletowa"**.

Nobody speaks English, so it's best to have the following phrase written down to show them.

I need a round trip bus ticket to the museum of the death camp Treblinka
Prosze bilet powrotny na autobus do muzeum obozu zaglady w Treblince

The bus will say **"Siedlce"** (the direction it's headed). The bus makes a Very Circuitous route (not the most direct) through the countryside stopping here and there to let people on and off. As always, have your destination Written Down to show the Driver when you board so they Know what stop you need. Sit in front if possible and most drivers will motion to you if they don't see you jumping up in time. Keep an eye out the window for signs (a Flame) pointing toward the camp site.

When you reach the site there is a Cement Marker on the Left side of the Road and a small sign on the Right pointing into the woods. The bus stop back is on the Left (circled below) in front of a house. It's a 10 minute walk down the road to the Right to the parking area (follow the signs) and paths into the camp site.

For better lighting this picture was taken from the opposite side of the road. These Markers are on the LEFT when coming from Malkinia.

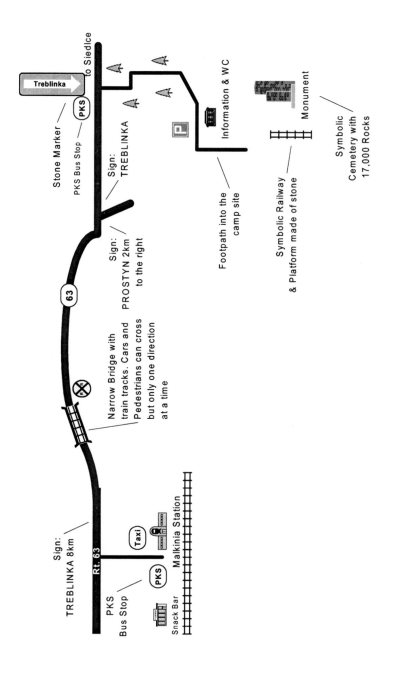

to Siedlce

Treblinka

PKS

Stone Marker

PKS Bus Stop

Sign:
TREBLINKA

Information & WC

Monument

Sign:
PROSTYN 2km
to the right

Footpath into the
camp site

Symbolic Railway
& Platform made of stone

Symbolic
Cemetery with
17,000 Rocks

63

Narrow Bridge with
train tracks. Cars and
Pedestrians can cross
but only one direction
at a time

Malkinia Station

Taxi

Sign:
TREBLINKA 8km

Rt. 63

PKS
Bus Stop

PKS

Snack Bar

TREBLINKA

To Walk:	**1 Hour & 40 minutes.** To walk you do NOT take the same circuitous route the bus takes. It's more of a straight shot in one direction but a long walk just the same. The Direct Road from Malkinia to Siedlce is **Route #63** Not far from the train station there is a direction sign for **Treblinka 8 km (5 miles).** It's a 2 lane country road, very few signs, a few farms & homes. No restrooms along the way. Exiting the train station walk straight back down the gravel road behind the station to the main road (Route #63) Not well marked. Turn Right. Follow this road all the way to Treblinka. The road twists and turns but it's all in the same direction. You will come to a very narrow bridge with train tracks going over it. Only one lane of cars can cross over at a time so they block it off. You may walk across when it's clear for cars to cross in your direction.

NOTE: See Website for Photos of this Bridge
www.scrapbookpages.com/Poland/Treblinka/Treblinka01.html

About 50 Minutes walk is the half way point. There is a side road to the Right that says Prostyn 2 km. There is also a sign pointing to Treblinka at that corner.
Do not turn here, keep going straight ahead. You will reach the Town of Treblinka. (Camp is another 4 km, 2.5 miles). Near the entrance you will see a Cement Marker **"Treblinka"** on the Left and a sign pointing down a narrow road to the Right.
It's about a 10 minute walk from here to the campsite.

By Car: Go Northeast on Hwy #18 from Warszawa to Ostrow Mazowiecka, then South on Hwy #63 toward Siedlce. Follow the signs.
It's 8km (5 miles) from Malkinia to the camp.
From the Town of Treblinka it's 4km, 2.5 miles

GUIDE SERVICE: Tomek Wisniewski
Email(s):   tomy@ld.euro-net.pl
    kolodno_holiday@yahoo.com
Website: www.kolodno-holiday.com/references.html
Tel/Fax: 48 +85 6634694
Mobile: 507 181939

Located in Bialystok, Poland. He offers friendly service and reasonable rates on comfortable mini-van tours, especially family tours to many of the Holocaust sites including: Treblinka, Bialystok Suwalki Lomza area, as well as entirely around Poland & Lithuania. He also does genealogical research in the archives in north east Poland & Lithuania.

What Remains:
Nothing that resembles a camp. There is a small building in the parking area with some weathered photos and descriptions of the camp site. Walk down the path following the signs. You will pass a few monument markers on the way to an area made up to resemble a train platform. To the left of that area is a huge field with a large monument and 17,000 stones, many of which have the names of towns chiseled into them.

There are signs pointing down the gravel path to Treblinka II labor camp. There is NOTHING down there to see. It takes about a half hour to walk down that lonely path. There is a marker and some crosses down there, nothing more. You might notice elderly people in the woods picking mushrooms.

Recommend: Due to the remoteness of this memorial (it' s in the middle of nowhere), the short time it will take to see the monuments, and amount of time it takes to reach by train, then bus, or foot, I highly suggest driving or taking an organized tour that includes this site.

Background:
Treblinka was the third of the extermination centers set up under "Operation (Aktion) Reinhardt. 13 Gas Chambers could handle 2000 at a time. Over 800,000 were killed here.
It was a very fast process. Approximately 2 hours after their arrival at the camp prisoners were gassed and bodies removed. An armed revolt by prisoners on August 2, 1943 resulted in the escape of some of the prisoners and shortly after the dismantling of the camp was started.

Camp Opened: 1942
Date Liquidated: July 1944

Treblinka Monument
with 17,000 memorial stones surrounding it

Majdanek

Address: Panstwowe Muzeum Na Majdanku
Droga Meczennikow Majdanka 67
20-325 Lublin

Phone: 48 + 81 + 74 426 47
FAX: 48 + 81 + 74 405 26

E-mail: archiwum@majdanek.pl
Webpage(s): www.majdanek.pl
www.scrapbookpages.com/Poland/Majdanek/Majdanek.html

Tour Guide: <u>East-West Guiding Agency in Lublin</u> see Page 191

Hours: <u>Parts of the Camp have Different Opening Times during the year:</u>

The Gas Chambers, Barracks #45 with a model of the camp, Barracks #52 & #53 with prisoners shoes, the 3rd prisoners field and the Crematorium
Open DAILY:
8am-3pm (October-April)
8am-6pm (May-September)

The Historical Exhibition "Majdanek" in Barracks #43 & #44
Open DAILY:
(except Mondays & religious/national holidays*)
8am-3pm (March-April and October-November)
8am-6pm (May-September)
Closed Dec 1 to Feb 28th,
but visiting arrangements can be made
by contacting the Museum's Section of Education
Tel: 48 + 81 + 74 419 55

Visitor Service Pavilion (next to the Monument)
Tel: +48-81-7441955
Information on guided tours, films, publications &
parking fees.
Open DAILY:
(except Mondays & religious/national holidays*)
8am-3pm (October-April)
8am-4pm (May-September)
Closed: Jan 1, Easter, May 1 & 3, Corpus
Christi, Aug 15, Nov 1 & 11, Dec 25-26.

Entrance: Free

Note: Children under the age of 14 are not admitted

Schedule: Plan on about 3 hours to visit this site.

Approx Train Travel Time to Lublin:

From:		
Berlin	11:50
Warsaw (Warszawa Centralna)	2:16
Krakow (Glowny)	4:25

By Train: From Warszawa (Warsaw), trains leave every few
hours for Lublin. The camp is approximately 4 km
(2½ miles) from the City Center.

To Walk: **40 Minutes.** From Lublin train station.
Exit the front of the station and turn Right.
You will be on **ul.Pocztowa**. When you reach the end
of that street you turn Right again and walk UNDER
the train track underpass.
You are now on **Wz.Kunickiego**. A few blocks down
you will cross the street and turn Left down **ul.Pawia**.
Stay on this street until it forks where you will
continue to the Left of the fork down **Lotnicza**.
The next Major intersection (not marked, but it's a
Major street with lots of traffic) is
Droga Meczennikow Majdanka. There is a Church
on the right hand corner and a gas station on the far
left corner. Turn Right (the camp is on this street) and
walk about 20 minutes to the camp site which will be
on the Right.

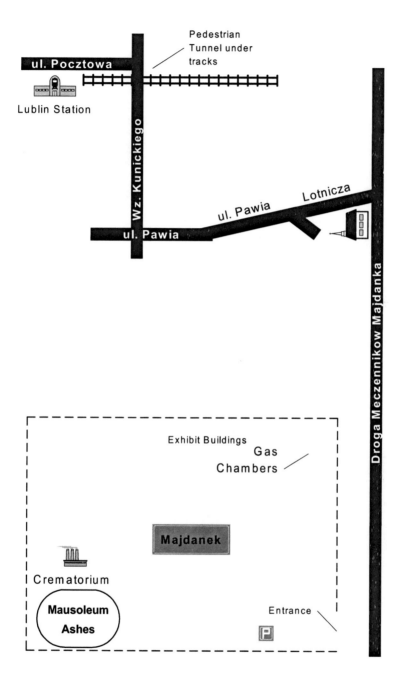

MAJDANEK

By Bus: Eastbound Bus #28 from the Train Station.
Trolley Buses #153, 156, 158 and Bus #23 from the
City Centre.

Monument in front of Majdanek Camp Entrance

Camp Opened: February 16, 1943
Date Liberated: July 22, 1944 by the Soviets

What Remains:
Gas chambers, crematorium ovens, and several buildings you can walk
through with thousands of pairs of shoes, empty Zyclon B gas cans, etc.

**Inside one of the
Gas Chambers.
Blue residue left from
the gas can still be
seen on the walls.**

The **Mausoleum**
a saucer-shaped
roof over a huge
mound of ashes
near the Crematorium

Sobibór

Address: Muzeum Byego Obozu Smierci w Sobiborze
Stacja Kolejowa 1
22-231 Sobibór, Poland

Phone: 48+82+ 57 19 867

Address:
For Info only Muzeum Pojezierza Leczynsko-Wlodawskiego (Sobibór)
ul. Czerwonego Krzyza 7
22-200 Wlodawa, Poland

Phone/Fax: 48+82+ 572 21 78

E-mail: mplw@wp.pl
Webpage(s): www.deathcamps.org
www.nizkor.org/faqs/reinhard

Hours: Daily 9:00-2:00 during the season 1st May-14th Oct.
Closed 15 Oct to 30 April

Entrance: Small Fee

Schedule: Plan on only about 30 minutes to see this site

Location: Near the village and railway station of Sobibór
in the eastern part of the Lublin District,
on the Chelm-Wlodawa railway line

Approx Train Travel Time to Sobibór:

From:		
Lublin	2:13
Belzec	4:00
Warsaw (Warszawa)	4:37
Krakow	10:09

By Train: NOT RECOMMENDED!
Sobibór train station is located right across the road
from the Camp museum, but there are VERY FEW
trains coming and going. You could end up spending
the whole day sitting there waiting for a train back.
Sobibór is located in the middle of nowhere in the
woods. Nothing around for miles.

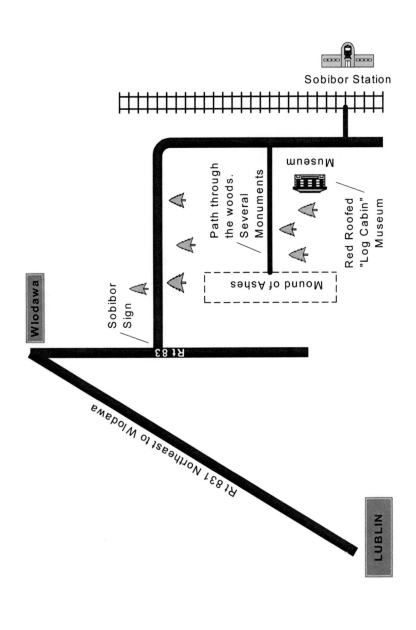

SOBIBóR

44

By Car: 1.5 Hours from Lublin. Take highway **#831** from Lublin to Wlodawa, then 9km (6 miles) south on highway **#83** to a turn off (marked by a sign) through the woods to Sobibór. Camp is located right across the road from the Train station.

By Bus: Lublin-Wlodawa-Sobibór

Recommend: Hire a Guide and Driver for the day. **East-West Guiding Agency in Lublin** see Page 191 can arrange the day for you. This way you will be driven there, see the site, have it explained to you and get you back in a few hours.

What Remains:
Nothing that resembles a camp. There is a small Red-Roofed Log Cabin Museum in front with a few exhibits. It is usually open during the days. Ring the bell if the door is locked. The gentleman that works there will guide you around the grounds and give you some information (in Polish, he does Not speak English). There are a few monuments down the path to the Right of the museum & a large monument of ashes in back.

Camp Opened: April 1942
Date Dismantled: October 20, 1943
(took until June 1944 to tear it down)

Background:
Sobibór was the second extermination camp set up under "Operation (Aktion) Reinhardt and used carbon monoxide from gas engines to murder the prisoners upon arrival. Estimated 250,000 Jews were murdered here. On 14th of October 1943 the prisoners revolted and fled into the woods. Of the hundreds who escaped, only about 50 survived the war. The others were captured and killed. After the escape Himmler ordered the camp dismantled without leaving a trace of what had happened there.

Recommended Viewing: Escape from Sobibór (1987)
Video & DVD   150 minutes

Recommended Reading: Escape from Sobibór
By Richard Rashke

Sobibór Museum
Across from the Train Station

Belzec

Address: **For Info Only**	Muzeum Regionalne (Belzec) ul. Zamojska 2 22-600 Tomaszów Lubelski, Poland
Phone: **Fax:**	None Available None Available
E-mail: **Webpage:**	None Available www.deathcamps.org www.nizkor.org/faqs/reinhard
Hours:	No Museum, so you may visit at any time.
Entrance:	Free
Schedule:	Plan on only about 30 minutes to see this site.
Location:	Southeastern part of the Lublin District, on the Lublin-Lvov railway line. Not far from the Ukrainian border.

Approx Train Travel Time to Belzec:

From:	Lublin	3:01
	Sobibór	4:00
	Krakow	7:20
	Warsaw (Warszawa)	8:39

By Train: NOT RECOMMENDED!
Very few trains coming and going. Although this area is not isolated in the woods like Sobibór, you would still end up having to spend many hours waiting for a return train to Lublin. Belzec Train station is about a 3 minute walk from the camp site. Exit the train and walk out to the main road (**Lwowska – Hwy 17** from Lublin).
Turn Left and walk about 3 minutes until you come to a rusty sign (a flame) pointing down a small road to the Left. You cross the train tracks and pass a house on the right and the camp gate is straight ahead.

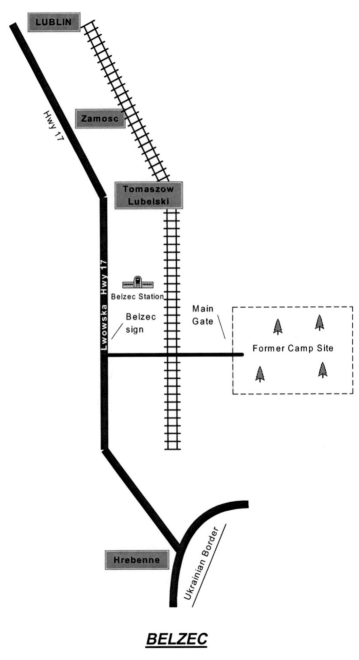

BELZEC

48

By Car: 1.5 Hours from Lublin South on **Highway #17**

By Bus: Lublin-Zamosc-Belzec

You travel through Zamosc and
Tomaszów Lubelski before reaching
Belzec. The camp is on the Left side
of the road just south of the Belzec
train station (also on the left).
Look for a rusty sign (a flame)
directing you to turn Left down a
small road across the train tracks
to the camp entrance.

Recommend: Hire a Guide and Driver for the day.
    East-West Guiding Agency in Lublin see Page 191
    can arrange the day for you. This way you will be
    driven there, see the site, have it explained to you
    and get you back in a few hours.

What Remains:
Nothing that resembles a camp. There is a memorial entrance gate.
A few descriptive signs (in Polish). Several small monuments and some
crumbling foundations in the woods. Nothing more.

Camp Opened: March 1942
Date Liquidated: June 1943

Background:
Belzec was the first of 3 extermination camps set up under
"Operation (Aktion) Reinhardt" Approximately 600,000 Jews were
murdered here using carbon monoxide from gas engines.

Chelmno (Kulmhof in German)

Address: Konin Museum (in charge of the Chelmno site)
For Info ul.Muzealna 6
Konin, Poland

Phone: 48+63+ 242-7530
48+63+ 242-7599
Fax: 48+63+ 242-7431

Email: Muzeumkn@kn.onet.pl
WebSite(s):
www.jewishgen.org/ForgottenCamps/Camps/ChelmnoEng.html
www.zchor.org/EDUT.HTM
http://weber.ucsd.edu/~lzamosc/gchelmno.html
http://weber.ucsd.edu/~lzamosc/gmoreinf.html

Address: Muzeum Bylego Obozu Zaglady
At the site Chelmno n/Nerem
62-663 Chelmno, Poland

Phone: 48+90+ 61 47 10

Hours: In Summer (Apr 1–Sep 30) Mon-Fri. 10:00-6:00
Sat-Sun 10:00-5:00
In Winter (Oct 1-Mar 31) Mon-Fri 8:00-2:00

Entrance: Free

Schedule: Plan on about 1 hour to see this site

Location: Located 47 miles (70 km) west of Lodz in the Kolo
District.

Approx Train Travel Time to Kolo
(Chelmno site is located between Kolo & Dabie)
From: Lodz 2:48
Poznan 2:17
Warsaw (Warszawa) 2:34
Krakow (Glowny) 5:00

By Train: The nearest train station is Kolo (pronounced *Ko-Wo*) on the route from Warszawa to Berlin. From Kolo you would need to either take a taxi or bus (15 km, 9 miles) to the former camp site.

By Bus: Exit Kolo station and it's about a 10 minute walk to the bus station. (bus stop in front of the train station is NOT the one you want).
Exit Kolo station which is on **KS Opalki.**
Walk straight ahead down **Kolejowa** for several blocks until you get to **Torunska** where you turn Left. The bus station **"PKS"** is a few steps down Torunska on the Left. The bus to Chelmno is traveling in the direction of Dabie (pronounced *Dome Bia*)

Regular bus service runs Monday-Friday
(Less Frequent Weekends)

Kolo-Chelmno-Dabie-Lodz
7:10, 10:10, 11:45, 12:40, 13:30, 15:20, 19:10

Chelmno-Kolo:
11:43, 11:57, 12:48, 14:18, 15:18, 16:42, 17:43

Chelmno-Lodz   (Lodz is pronounced *Wooch*)
8:59, 10:33, 12:08, 13:03, 13:53, 15:42, 17:22

There is a bus stop across from the Museum of Chelmno.
This is in the middle of a forest.

The museum is a white building on the Right side of the road slightly back and out of sight until you get right to it.

As Always, Write Down where you are going and show the Driver. Sit up front on the Right side if possible and hopefully they will let you know when to get off.

The bus stop nearest the Excavation Site is another 6 km (4 miles) further south just past the excavation site itself. Knowing when to exit the bus will be difficult unless you keep an eye out the window for a sign. The bus passes the

small building on the Right that houses the artifacts and past a white Church on the right and then stops at the bus stop

From there walk BACK north about 5 minutes to that driveway into the dig site. When finished there, either walk north on that same road (about 6km, 4 miles) to the Museum or back to the bus stop.

By Car: Take Highway **A2** (Main highway between Warszawa & Poznan) to Kolo and South on Highway **#473**, 12 km (7½ miles) to the site (see map)

Recommend: Arrange for a driver and guide, especially if you want to see the excavation site. It is marked with signs, but would be easier to visualize with a guide helping to explain what you are seeing. If just going to the museum and surrounding monuments, you could do that easily on your own.

Boxes of artifacts found at the dig site. The Nazis buried everything to try and hide their crimes. Toys, clothes, teeth, combs, jewelry etc. All this found just below the surface.

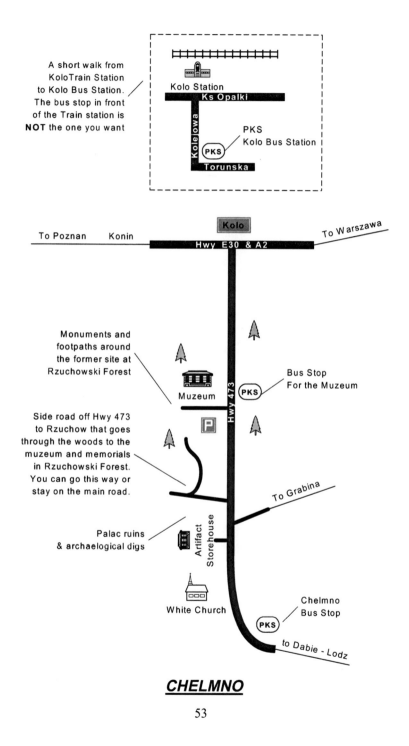

A short walk from KoloTrain Station to Kolo Bus Station. The bus stop in front of the Train station is **NOT** the one you want

Kolo Station

Ks Opalki

Koleiowa

PKS

PKS Kolo Bus Station

Torunska

To Poznan   Konin

Kolo

To Warszawa

Hwy E30 & A2

Monuments and footpaths around the former site at Rzuchowski Forest

Muzeum

Hwy 473

PKS

Bus Stop For the Muzeum

Side road off Hwy 473 to Rzuchow that goes through the woods to the muzeum and memorials in Rzuchowski Forest. You can go this way or stay on the main road.

P

To Grabina

Palac ruins & archaelogical digs

Artifact Storehouse

White Church

Chelmno Bus Stop

PKS

to Dabie - Lodz

CHELMNO

What Remains:

At Rzuchowski Forest Site: (9km, 5½ miles from Kolo)

A museum with information (in Polish) about what happened at
Rzuchowski (pronounced *Zoo hof ski*) Forest and Chelmno Camp.
Several monuments scattered around the area.
A few partial ruins of a crematorium and building foundations.

2 monuments near the Chelmno Museum in Rzuchowski Forest

At the Excavation Site: (12km, 7½ miles from Kolo)

Excavations in the ground which have uncovered many artifacts from
the victims: such as jewelry, clothes, teeth, bones, toys etc.

**Dig site of the *Palac* where
victims were gassed in vans.
The white Church in the back
is the one you pass on the way
to the Bus stop.**

Teeth found at the dig site.

Camp Opened: December 1941
Date Liberated: January 18, 1945

54

Gross-Rosen (Rogoznica)

Address: Panstwowe Muzeum Gross-Rosen w Rogoznica
58-152 Goczalkow
Woj. Walbrzyskie, Poland

Phone: 48+74+ 855-90-07

Archives & Scientific-Research Studies
ul. Starachowicka 9a
58-300 Walbrzych, ul. Szarych Szeregów 9
skr. poczt. 217

Phone: 48+74+ 842-15-80
Fax: 48+74+ 842-15-94

E-mail: muzeum@gross-rosen.pl *or* pmgr@wb.onet.pl
WebPage(s):   www.gross-rosen.pl
www.geocities.com/Pentagon/7087/uk025.htm

Hours: Daily
October 16 to March 15   8am-5pm
March 16 to April 30   8am-6pm
May 1 to August 31   8am-8pm
September 1 to October 15   8am-6pm

Entrance: Free

Guide Service Available for a Minimal Charge

Note: Children under the age of 13 are not allowed to visit Museums of Martyrdom. (This is not strictly enforced)

Schedule: Plan on about 1 hour to see this site

Location: Near the town of Rogoznica (between Legnica & Swidnica). Camp is about 3 km – 2 miles Southwest of Rogoznica station on a road to Roztoka. Rogoznica is situated 12 km-7 mi from Strzegom en route from Strzegom to Legnica on Hwy #374

Approx Train Travel Time to Rogoznica (Gross-Rosen):

From:

Berlin	8:37
Gdansk (Glowny)	8:24
Krakow (Glowny)	7.19
Warsaw (Warszawa)	8:11
Prague (Praha hl.n)	9.45

By Train: You will most likely be coming from Wroclaw (pronounced *Vrots waf*) if taking the train. Rogoznica train station is about 60km (37 miles) southwest of Wroclaw in Southwest Poland near the Czech border. This is a VERY small station with no facilities. No lockers for baggage and only a few trains stop here. There are no buses to the camp site from this station, and not a taxi in sight.

To Walk: **45 Minutes**. From Rogoznica train station exit the back of the station and turn Right down that road. When you get to the corner, turn Left and walk to the main road (Rt. 374), about 4 minutes, and turn Left. Cross the Street and you will see a Blue sign

"Muzeum Gross-Rosen" directing you to the Right.

It's about a 25 minute walk down that road, keeping to the Left when you get to the fork in the road.

It's marked with signs.

The camp will be on the Right side of the road. You reach a stone quarry and a sign that says "Gross-Rosen II". This is NOT the camp site. Keep walking until you get to the Camp Memorial and Museum entrance on the Right.

By Bus: There is a Bus Stop in front of the camp entrance. The bus that stops here comes from Strezgdom. Most tourists would not be traveling from there.

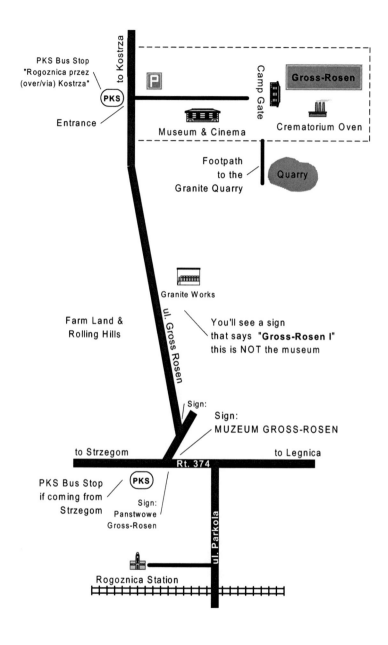

to Kostrza

PKS Bus Stop
"Rogoznica przez
(over/via) Kostrza"

PKS

Entrance

P

Museum & Cinema

Camp Gate

Gross-Rosen

Crematorium Oven

Footpath
to the
Granite Quarry

Quarry

Granite Works

ul. Gross Rosen

Farm Land &
Rolling Hills

You'll see a sign
that says **"Gross-Rosen I"**
this is NOT the museum

Sign:

Sign:
MUZEUM GROSS-ROSEN

to Strzegom

to Legnica

Rt. 374

PKS Bus Stop
if coming from
Strzegom

PKS

Sign:
Panstwowe
Gross-Rosen

ul. Parkola

Rogoznica Station

GROSS-ROSEN

By Car: Take Highway #374 (Look for signs)
Camp is halfway between Legnica & Swidnica.

What Remains:
Main gate, several buildings, small crematorium oven, foundations of buildings, museum with a few exhibits. Cinema.

Stone markers at the entrance to the camp

Main Gate and Guard Tower at Gross-Rosen

View of the camp from the top of the guard tower

Camp Opened: Aug 1940 as a sub-camp of Sachsenhausen.
May 1, 1941 as a separate concentration camp

Date Liberated: February 13, 1945 by the Russian soldiers of 70th Brigade

GERMANY

BERLIN Area

Approx Train Travel Time to Berlin:

From:

Amsterdam	8:19
Munich (München)	8:19
Krakow	10:07
Warsaw (Warszawa)	8:33
Weimar	3:29
Hamburg	2:40

Webpage(s):

Berlin S-Bahn & U-Bahn
http://de.geocities.com/metroplanet_berlin/berlin.htm
www.bvg.de/e_index.html

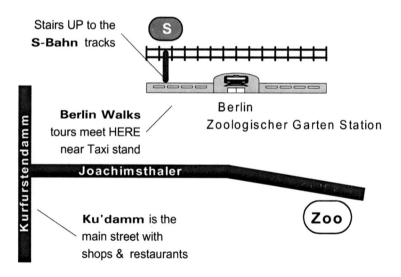

Stairs UP to the **S-Bahn** tracks

Berlin Walks tours meet HERE near Taxi stand

Berlin Zoologischer Garten Station

Kurfurstendamm

Joachimsthaler

Ku'damm is the main street with shops & restaurants

Zoo

Berlin Zoologischer Garten Train Station
Across the street from the Berlin Zoo (one of the Best!)

(Third Reich Sites) I recommend the *"BERLIN WALKS"* tours. They are very informative and an inexpensive way to see the city & ask questions. They meet in front of the Berlin Zoo Rail Station near the Taxi stand, Daily* around 10am for their City Walks, one of which is:

"INFAMOUS THIRD REICH SITES"

This covers many of the Third Reich's Buildings, History of the SS, part of the Berlin Wall, and ends up at the site of Hitler's Bunker (which is buried near an apartment building parking area & is NOT accessible)

(No prior booking is required to take the tours, just show up*)

April:	Saturdays & Sundays at 10am
May thru Sept:	Wed., Fri., Sat & Sun. at 10am
October:	Saturdays & Sundays at 10am

They also have a tour to **Sachsenhausen Concentration Camp**

April:	Tuesdays & Saturdays at 10.15am
May thru Sept:	Tues., Thurs., Sat. & Sun. at 10.15am
October:	Tuesdays & Saturdays at 10.15am

* Check their website for current schedules as they are subject to change.
They also have other great tours that run Daily year round

WebSite: www.berlinwalks.com
E-Mail: berlin.walks@snafu.de
Phone: 49+30 301-9194

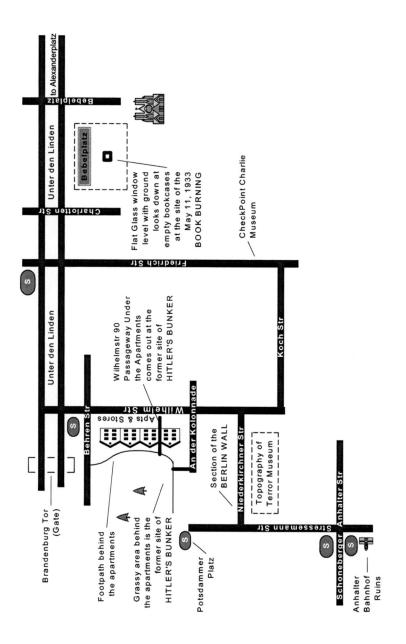

BERLIN

Sachsenhausen-Oranienburg

Address: Stiftung Brandenburgische Gedenkstätten
                  Strasse der Nationen 22
                  16515 Oranienburg, Germany

Phone: 49 + 03301 / 803715
Fax: 49 + 03301 / 803718

E-mail: None Available
Webpage(s):   www.gedenkstaette-sachsenhausen.de (in German only)
www.jewishgen.org/ForgottenCamps/Camps/SachsenhausenEng.html

Hours: 8:30am-4:30pm Tue-Sun October 1 to March 31
                  8:30am-6:00pm Tue-Sun April 1 to Sept. 30
                  CLOSED on MONDAYS

Entrance: Free

Schedule: Plan on at least 2 hours to see it all.

Location: 1 Hour train ride North of the Berlin Zoo Station.

By Train: From Berlin Zoo Station take any one of these
                  S-Bahn trains to Friedrichstrasse
                  S3 Erkner   **S5** Strausberg Nord
                  S7 Ahrensfelde   **S9** Berlin Schonefeld
                  Change at Friedrichstr. to the **S1** to Oranienburg
                  Do NOT get off at "Oranienburger Str" which is an
                  S-Bahn stop in Berlin one stop north of Friedrichstr.
                  Continue on to "Oranienburg"

Berlin S-Bahn & U-Bahn
          http://de.geocities.com/metroplanet_berlin/berlin.htm
          www.bvg.de/e_index.html

(**Note:** Eurailpasses are valid on S-Bahn Trains but not U-Bahn)

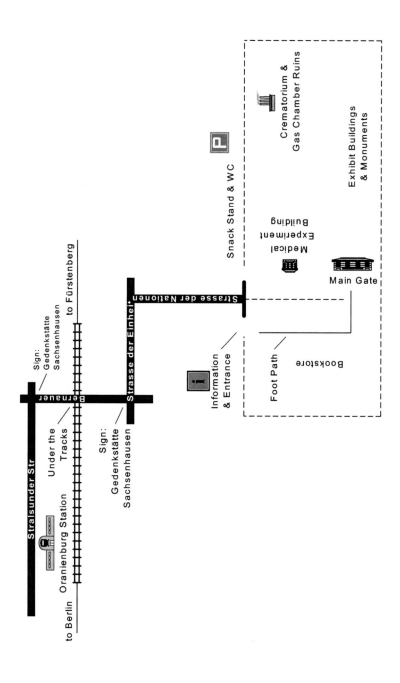

SACHSENHAUSEN

To Walk: **20 Minutes** from Oranienburg station. Exit the Oranienburg station and turn RIGHT (you will be on Stralsunder Strasse). Walk down that street until you reach Bernauer Strasse. Turn Right (you'll see a sign directing you to Gedenkstätte Sachsenhausen).

Gedenkstätte (pronounced *Ga Dane Schtetta*) means Memorial

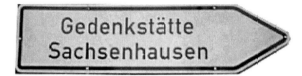

You walk under a railway overpass.
Continue down this street until you come to Strasse der Einheit and turn Left (there is a sign there also).
Walk down that street until you come to Strasse der Nationen and turn Right.

This is a tree-lined residential street, at the end of which is the camp entrance.

Entry to the camp is Free but be sure to ask for a English pamphlet (small fee) at the entrance building window (circled below)

Entrance to Sachsenhausen

By Car: Take the A111 in the direction of Hamburg. At the Oranienburg junction take the A10 towards Prenzlau. Take the Birkenwerder exit to B96 in the direction of Oranienburg then follow the signs to **(Gedenkstätte Sachsenhausen)**

What Remains:

Many excellent exhibits, crematorium & gas chamber ruins, medical experimentation room, prison cells and memorials.

Main Gate to the Camp

Pathology Building. Medical Experiments were carried out here.

Lamp Shades were made from the Tattooed skin of prisoners.

Camp Opened: 1936
Date Liberated: April 22, 1945

Ravensbrück

Address: Mahn und Gedenkstätte Ravensbruck
                  Strase der Nationen
                  D-16798 Furstenberg Germany

Phone: 49+33093-608-0
Fax: 49+33093-608-29

E-mail: info@ravensbrueck.de
WebSite: www.ravensbrueck.de

Hours: Tuesday-Sunday 9:00am-5:00pm.
                  CLOSED on MONDAYS

Entrance: Free

Schedule: Plan on about 2 Hours to tour this camp site.

Location: 87km (54 miles) North of Berlin, about a half hour
                  further north of Sachsenhausen Camp.
                  You can easily see BOTH of these camps in one day
                  if you start early in the morning.

By Train: To reach the camp you will be taking a train from
                  Berlin's Zoolg. Garten (Main) station.
                  (across from the Berlin Zoo, one of the Best!).
                  The train you want to take is one that stops at
                  "Fürstenberg Havel" station. It's approximately 1 hour
                  journey time. If you visit this camp early in the
                  morning, you can stop at Oranienburg and visit
                  Sachsenhausen on the return to Berlin.

To Walk: **40 Minutes** walk from the Fürstenberg Havel train
                  station. (3 km – 2 miles) Exit Fürstenberg Station and
                  turn Left down that street (Luisenstrasse).

The first street you
come to you'll see a
Sign on the Light Post
pointing the way to
RAVENSBRÜCK.

Turn right down this street (Rathenaustrasse) and go all the way down to the end which will be Unter den Linden (Highway 96 & E251). Turn Left on Unter den Linden.

A couple blocks down you'll be making a Right Turn (look for RAVENSBRÜCK SIGN) down Dorfstrasse. Walk down that street following signs which will lead you to a fork in the road where you'll bear to the Right down Strasse der Nationen which leads directly into the camp.

You'll notice what appears to be a vacant supermarket on your Right. That is exactly what it is. They built this right near the entrance to the camp and there was such outrage that it was never opened. Also along this street you'll see boarded up houses. These were formerly SS officers and guards homes. The Soviets took over these homes after the war, and now most of them are left in disrepair.

By Car: Take the B96 from Berlin in the direction of Fürstenberg-Neustrelitz-Stralsund.

Once in Fürstenberg
follow the signs
"Gedenkstätte Ravensbrück"

Monument on Dorfstrasse on the way to Ravensbrück Camp.

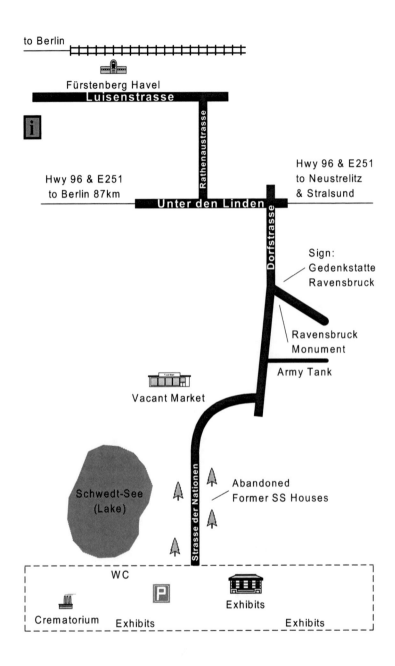

to Berlin

Fürstenberg Havel
Luisenstrasse

Rathenaustrasse

Hwy 96 & E251
to Berlin 87km

Unter den Linden

Dorfstrasse

Hwy 96 & E251
to Neustrelitz
& Stralsund

Sign:
Gedenkstatte
Ravensbruck

Ravensbruck
Monument

Army Tank

Vacant Market

Schwedt-See
(Lake)

Strasse der Nationen

Abandoned
Former SS Houses

WC

Crematorium   Exhibits

P

Exhibits

Exhibits

RAVENSBRÜCK

What Remains:

There is not too much to see at Ravensbrück. Only a small portion of the camp is open to the public. It is located in what once was the Eastern Bloc and was left in ruin for many years. It has since been cleaned up somewhat and has a few buildings and a crematorium for people to visit. This was primarily a women's camp, not necessarily Jews, but many people who helped in the resistance movement (such as Corrie Ten Boom and her sister who hid people in their secret *Hiding Place*).

Crematorium

Monument near the entrance to the Crematorium

Camp Opened: Spring of 1939
Date Liberated: April 30, 1945
by the Red Army

69

House of the Wannsee Conference
(Haus der Wannsee Konferenz)

Address: Am Grossen Wannsee 56-58
D-14109 Berlin, Germany

Phone: 49+30-805001 20
Fax: 49+30-805001 27

E-mail: info@ghwk.de
Webpage(s): www.ghwk.de/engl/kopfengl.htm
http://historyplace.com/worldwar2/timeline/wannsee2.htm

Hours: Open Daily 10-6 (Closed on Holidays – see website)

Entrance: Free

Schedule: Plan on at least 1 hour to see this museum.

Location: In the Wannsee Lake area of Berlin,
a short distance south of downtown Berlin.

By Train: Take the S-Bahn (**S3** or **S7**) from the Berlin Zoo
Station in the direction of Potsdam Stadt.
The Wannsee stop is about 4 stops before Potsdam.

Berlin S-Bahn & U-Bahn
http://de.geocities.com/metroplanet_berlin/berlin.htm
www.bvg.de/e_index.html

(**Note:** Eurailpasses are valid on S-Bahn Trains but not U-Bahn)

To Walk: <u>40 Minute</u> walk to the Mansion (down a nice tree
lined residential area along the lake).
I enjoy walking & always like to get to places by foot
to see more of the area.
The Train Station is on **Kronprinzessinnenweg**
If you left the train tracks and went to the Right
(under the street) you would come up across the street
from the Train Station and turn RIGHT.
If you went into the Terminal, you will come out of
the station and walk to the Left.

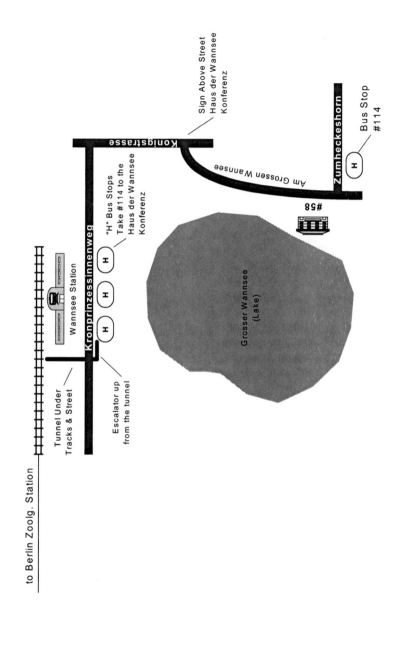

Map labels:
- to Berlin Zoolg. Station
- Tunnel Under Tracks & Street
- Wannsee Station
- Kronprinzessinnenweg
- Escalator up from the tunnel
- "H" Bus Stops Take #114 to the Haus der Wannsee Konferenz
- Königstrasse
- Sign Above Street Haus der Wannsee Konferenz
- Am Grossen Wannsee
- Grosser Wannsee (Lake)
- #58
- Zumheckeshorn
- Bus Stop #114

HOUSE of the WANNSEE CONFERENCE
(Haus der Wannsee Konferenz)

71

The LAKE will be on the RIGHT side of the street either way. Walk down that street to the first intersection which is **Konigstrasse** and turn RIGHT. Walk down that street quite a ways until you see a sign in the Middle of the road that says **"Haus der Wannsee Konferenz"** pointing to the Right down **Am Grossen Wannsee**. Walk to the Right down that street passing a lot of very nice old houses **(the lake will ALWAYS be on your Right)** You are looking for **#58**. Once in front of #58 you'll see it's Gated but there is a Doorbell on the wall. Ring the Middle Bell (marked Gedenkstätte) and they will BUZZ you in. Walk up to the Front Door & AGAIN Ring the Bell and they'll BUZZ you in.

By Bus:

From the Wannsee S-Bahn station cross the street (be on the lake side) take Bus #114 to the house. It makes a loop & returns back to the station so don't worry about going in the wrong direction. The bus Passes the house and immediately turns Left and stops at the bus stop on the corner of Zumheckeshorn within sight of the house. (see MAP)

Background:

This is the mansion in a Berlin suburb where on January 20th, 1942, Heydrich, Eichmann & 13 others met to plan the implementation of **"The Final Solution to the Jewish Question"**, which, of course, was how to ship all these people to camps and murder them. It is an EXCELLENT museum with pictures showing the whole process from start to finish. (Most documentation is in German Only, but if you have studied the Holocaust and know a little German the pictures & descriptions will be self explanatory)

Recommended Viewing: Conspiracy (2001)
Kenneth Branagh 96 minutes

Ring the Middle bell
marked Gedenkstätte
And they will
Buzz You In!

#58 Front Gate of the House of the Wannsee Conference

Topography of Terror
(Stiftung Topographie des Terrors)

Address: Niederkirchnerstrase 8
                   10963 Berlin

Phone: 49+30-254 86 703
Fax: 49+30-262 71 56

E-mail: info@topographie.de
WebSite: www.topographie.de/en

Hours: Open Daily October-April 10:00am-6:00pm
                              May-September 10:00am-8:00pm

Entrance: Free

Schedule: Plan on about 15 minutes to view this site,
                   longer once the permanent exhibit opens.

Location: Berlin

S-Bahn: Anhalter Bahnhof or Potsdamer Platz
U-Bahn: Kochstrasse
By Bus: Numbers 248, 341, 129

To Walk: **(See Berlin Map Page 61)**
                   From the S-Bahn Stop at Anhalter Bahnhof,
                   when you come up to street level go Left
                   down Stressemann Str. until you reach
                   Niederkirchner Str. (just a few blocks)
                   Turn Right down Niederkirchner Str. and the
                   Museum area and portion of the Berlin Wall
                   will be clearly visible on the Right.

What to See: This is a museum set up on the Prince Albrecht Site in
                   Berlin's Kreuzberg district, which was the former
                   headquarters of the Gestapo, SS and Reich Security
                   Main Office. Pictures and documentation showing the
                   Nazis rise to power and the Third Reich in action are
                   displayed here in a temporary outdoor exhibit while
                   construction of a permanent exhibit is planned.

Temporary Outdoor Exhibit: The Topography of Terror Museum

Berlin Wall

Webpage(s)   http://userpage.chemie.fu-berlin.de/BIW/wall.html
http://www.wall-berlin.org/gb/berlin.htm

One of the sections of the Berlin Wall remaining as a reminder of the
Cold War is located right behind the Topography of Terror's temporary
outdoor exhibit pictured Above.

**A section of
the Berlin
Wall**

Checkpoint Charlie

Former Checkpoint Crossing into
East Berlin. There is a museum,
HAUS AM CHECKPOINT CHARLIE
open Daily 9am-10pm, located at the site
on Friedrich Str. near Koch Str.
(See Berlin Map Page 61)

Website(s):
www.dailysoft.com/berlinwall/checkpoint-charlie.htm

Bebelplatz (Site of the Nazi Book Burning)

This is the spot where on May 10, 1933, books by Jewish authors and many others were burned. The Nazis were starting their campaign to erase the Jewish culture from German life and anything else that they felt threatened their cause.

In the center of this square is a glass window looking down into a room with empty bookcases. It's a thought provoking memorial to that night.

See Map of Berlin on Page 61 for the location.
It's right on Unter den Linden near the Opera House. You can't really see this glass window from the street since it's flat to the ground.

Walk into the middle of the square where you will most likely see people standing looking down at something and taking pictures.

NOTE:
Construction in this area during 2003-2004 may make it impossible to see the memorial.

Website(s):
http://fcit.coedu.usf.edu/holocaust/gallery/01622.htm
http://historyplace.com/worldwar2/timeline/bookburn.htm

Glass window looking down into Empty Bookcases

Bebelplatz (Site of Nazi Bookburning)

See people standing in the middle of the picture. That's where the Window Is!

Hitler's Bunker Site

See Map of Berlin Page 61 for location.
The war was lost and Hitler knew it. So rather than face the consequences he committed suicide along with his wife of only a few hours, Eva Braun. Several of his top brass also took this cowardly way out. Deep down they must have known what they were doing to the Jews was criminal and they'd have to answer for it.

To avoid having his Bunker turned into some sort of shrine for neo Nazi groups, it was decided to destroy it and leave it buried.
There are no markers showing the spot. It is located behind a playground area in back of some apartment buildings.
There is nothing to see there but the empty field and playground.

Website: www.xs4all.nl/~odu/bunker.html

Site of Hitler's Bunker

At Wilhelmstrasse 90 there is a passageway under the apartment complex in between some stores. It comes out at the playground area.

Bergen-Belsen

Address:	Gedenkstätte Bergen-Belsen D-29303 Lohheide Germany
Phone:	49+ 5051 6011
Fax:	49+ 5051 7396
E-mail:	Bergen-Belsen@t-online.de
Webpage:	www.bergenbelsen.de/en/index.php
Hours:	Open Daily 9:00am-6:00pm Closed Dec. 24th, 25th, 26th & 31st and Jan. 1st
Entrance:	Free
Schedule:	Plan on about 2 hours to see this site. If you are coming by bus, you will be there from around 1pm until almost 5pm when the only bus back departs. That is more than ample time to take it slow and walk around.
Location:	South of Hamburg near the town of Bergen.

Approx Train Travel Time to Celle:

From:		
Berlin	3:30
Amsterdam	5:00
Munich (München)	7:51
Hamburg	1:12

By Train: The Nearest train station is Celle. From there you need to take a bus or taxi (about 45 minutes).

By Bus: Exit the front of Celle train station & turn Left
Look for **"H"** (denotes bus stops in Germany)
The Bus for Bergen-Belsen is **#9**
You may pay the driver, they make change.

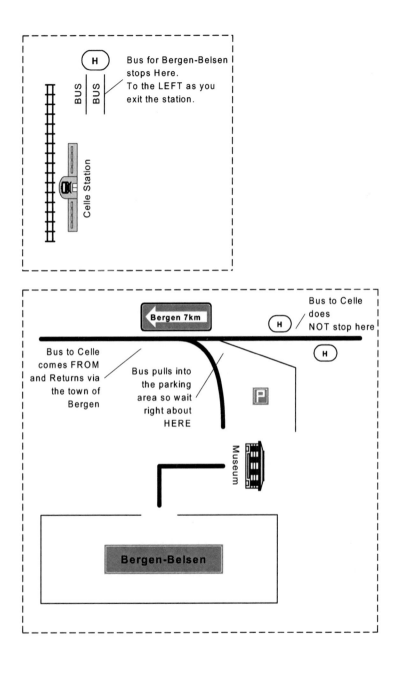

Bus for Bergen-Belsen stops Here.
To the LEFT as you exit the station.

BUS | BUS

Celle Station

Bergen 7km

Bus to Celle does NOT stop here

Bus to Celle comes FROM and Returns via the town of Bergen

Bus pulls into the parking area so wait right about HERE

Museum

Bergen-Belsen

BERGEN-BELSEN

Note: Be sure to write down **"Gedenkstätte Bergen-Belsen"** and show it to the driver as you buy your ticket. The reason I say this is because if no one is going to the camp site, they will sometimes NOT STOP THERE since it's out of the way. You might be the only one going there so be sure the driver knows *In Advance* where you are going.

DON'T PANIC if you notice the driver goes past the turn off for Bergen-Belsen. The bus makes a very circuitous route through the town of Bergen before working its way to the camp. The bus pulls right into the camp parking lot.

IMPORTANT:
The Bus also pulls into the camp parking lot when picking people up. There are bus stops out on the road, but the bus does NOT stop there! When leaving, stand near the entrance of the camp within sight of the bus stops on the road and the entrance to the museum. The bus will pull in and stop right about there to pick you up. (see Map) The bus comes from the direction of Bergen and goes back the same way. If you are looking for the bus and are walking OUT of the camp entrance, it will be coming from the Left from the town of Bergen.

BUS SCHEDULE
Celle Bahnhof to Gedenkstätte Bergen-Belsen
(approximately 45 minute ride)

12:05pm Monday though Friday
13:40 Monday through Friday (only on schooldays)

Gedenkstätte Bergen-Belsen to Celle Bahnhof
16:54 & 17:34 Monday through Friday

NO BUSES ON SATURDAYS or SUNDAYS

By Car: From Celle, take the B3 toward Hamburg to

Hinweisschild (20 km, 12½ miles from Celle) turn left and continue straight to Bergen-Belsen, following the "Gedenkstätte" (memorial) signs.

What Remains:

Nothing that resembles a camp. There is a small museum with exhibits. Two Cinema rooms. Check the sign for the times of the English version of the film. (Free entrance). It is about 30 minutes long & well worth seeing.

On the grounds there are the mass graves marked with cement notices "5000" Here, "2500" Here.

The captured Nazi Guards were forced to help with the dirty work of burying the dead. There are a few monuments, some broken foundations of buildings in the woods and some excavations deeper in the woods to the right of where you came in. Walk along the paths following the directions shown on the free brochures available in several different languages.

1000 Here

All of the barracks were burned to contain Typhus at the end of the war

Point of Interest: This is the camp where Anne Frank died about a month before liberation.

Camp Opened: April 1943   **Date Liberated:** April 15, 1945

Neuengamme

Address: Jean-Dolidier-Weg 39
D-21039 Hamburg, Germany

Phone: 49+40-428 96 03
Fax: 49+40-428 96 525

Email: info@kz-gedenkstaette-neuengamme.de
WebPage(s): www.hamburg.de/Neuengamme/welcome.en.html

Hours: April to Sept: Tues-Fri. 10am-5pm, Sat-Sun. 10-6pm
October to March Tues-Sun. 10am-5pm
CLOSED MONDAYS

Entrance: Free

Schedule: Plan on about 2 hours to see this site.

Location: A short distance southeast of Hamburg.

Approx Train Travel Time to Hamburg:
From:

Berlin	2:29
Munich (München)	8:41
Amsterdam	5:59
Celle	1:12
Weimar	5:13

By Train: The nearest train station is Hamburg
where you will then take the S-Bahn train.

Hamburg S-Bahn & U-Bahn
www.metropla.net/eu/ham/hamburg.htm

By S-Bahn: From Hamburg Hbf (main train station) take the
S-Bahn to Bergedorf (Look for the **S2** or **S21**
direction of Bergedorf or Friedrichsruh)
(about 20 minutes travel time).

S-Bahn platforms are downstairs inside the Hamburg station. Trains run every few minutes. From Bergedorf you will take a bus to the camp.

Note: Euroilpasses are Valid on S-Bahn trains, but Not the U-Bahn.
If you don't have a pass and need to purchase an S-Bahn ticket there are machines in the station.

By Bus: Exit the front of Bergedorf S-Bahn station.
You will see rows of bus stops (marked **"H"**)

You want the bus stop Farthest from the building & located ON THE STREET. Bus **#227** goes to Neuengamme. You may pay the driver, they make change.

It's approximately 40 minutes to the stop for the Neuengamme camp. As always, write down the name of where you are going **"KZ Gedenkstätte Neuengamme"** to show the driver. After about 20 minutes the bus reaches a stop for Jean-Dolidier-Weg (camp is located on this street) You *CAN* get off here (there are signs) and walk to the Right down Jean-Dolidier-Weg about 5 minutes to the camp which will be on the Left, OR, stay on the bus. It reaches a main road which runs parallel to a river, then turns right and winds it's way back to Jean-Dolidier-Weg and the KZ Neuengamme stop after about 15 minutes.

BUS SCHEDULE:
Bergedorf S-Bahn to KZ Neuengamme
Tues.-Sat.   9:42, 10:42, 11:42 etc
Sun. & Holidays 9:35, 10:35, 11:35 etc

KZ Neuengamme to Bergedorf S-Bahn
Tues.-Sat.   10:16, 11:16, 12:16 etc
Sun. & Holidays 10:09, 11:09, 12:09 etc

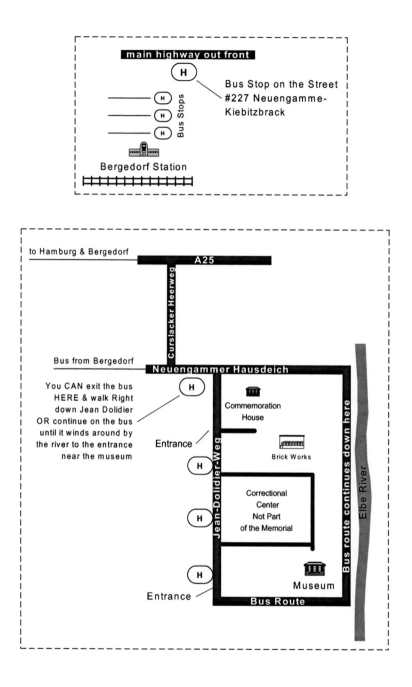

NEUENGAMME

By Car: Take Highway A25 in the direction of Geesthacht.
Exit at Curslack and follow the signs from there.

What Remains:

Not very much. Neuengamme (pronounced: *Noy in gamma*) has a small
museum with exhibits, films, slide shows, and several other buildings on
the grounds as you wind your way through the site.
There is NOT a lot to see here.
There is only one of the brick works building open, and it just looks like
a huge empty warehouse. There are a couple of informational
boards inside that look like they've been neglected for years.

**Pickup a free brochure/map on your way in & follow the "Circuit"
(dotted lines on the map) to lead you around the grounds.**

It's all rather confusing because there is an actual working prison on the
grounds out front and what is left of the camp winds around back and
between it.

Recommend: Stay on the bus until it winds around to the other
entrance to the area (see map page 85)
The reason I say this is because the entrance you
would go to if you get off the bus when it reaches
Jean Dolidier Weg has a small Commemoration
House (and those brochures/map) but this building is
not always open and without the brochure, you won't
have a clue about which way to walk or what you are
seeing. There are some signs, but that prison in the
middle makes it confusing.

At the entrance by the Commemoration House.
Paths lead from here to memorials in the nearby field
and to the Brick Works. (Below)

Prisoners had to work making bricks in these buildings.
Working conditions were terrible, many died from
exhaustion, illness and lack of food or were simply killed
when they could no longer serve a purpose for the SS.

Camp Opened: Summer of 1940
Date Evacuated: Early 1945

Bullenhuser Damm Memorial

Address: Bullenhuser Damm 92
             20539 Hamburg, Germany

Phone: 49+40-428 96 03   (Neuengamme Museum has info)
Fax: 49+40-428 96 525

E-mail: info@kz-gedenkstaette-neuengamme.de
Webpage:
        www.hamburg.de/Neuengamme/bullenhuserdamm.en.html

Hours: Sunday   10:00-5:00
             Thursday   2:00-8:00
             and by appointment

             The outdoor Rose Garden area is open 24 hours

Entrance: Free

Schedule: Plan on about 5 minutes to see the memorial rooms
             and another 5 minutes in the Rose Garden.

Hamburg S-Bahn & U-Bahn
        www.metropla.net/eu/ham/hamburg.htm

By S-Bahn: From Hamburg Hbf (Hauptbahnhof/Main Station)
             Note: Eurailpasses are Valid on S-Bahn trains,
                 but not U-Bahn.
             If you don't have a pass and need to purchase an
             S-Bahn ticket there are machines in the station.
             Go downstairs to the S-Bahn platforms.
             Take the **S2** or **S21** in the direction of Bergedorf or
             Friedrichsruh.
             Exit at Rothenburgsort (about 5 minutes)

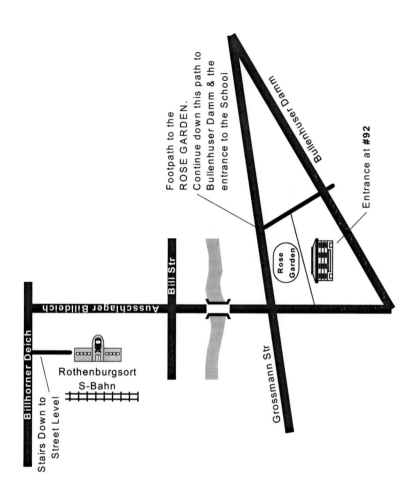

BULLENHUSER DAMM MEMORIAL

To Walk: **5 Minutes.** Exit Rothenburgsort S-Bahn station and walk down the stairs to street level and immediately turn Right. You will be on Billhorner Deich. At the next corner turn Right again down Ausschläger Billdeich. Walk straight ahead, crossing Bill Strasse. Cross over the bridge and at the next major intersection, Grossmann Str. you will see the large brown school on the far left corner behind a fence and trees.

Cross over to this corner (see map) and walk to the Left until you come to an entrance in the fence.

This is where the memorial **Rose Garden** is located.

Continue down the footpath outside the Rose Garden Entrance to the street in front of the school which is on "Bullenhuser Damm".

There are two entrances, you want the first one on the right marked #92.

Walk upstairs, go inside and turn Left and walk Downstairs.
Turn Right and again walk Downstairs into the Basement.
This is the memorial room.

What Remains:
Very little to see. There is a Gedenkstätte (Memorial) in a small area of the basement of this school building.
A few explanations (in German) on the walls.
A Rose Garden behind the school in memory of those murdered here.

Background:
This was a former school building on the Bullenhuser Damm in Hamburg. In October of 1944, it became a subcamp of KZ Neuengamme concentration camp.
At the Neuengamme camp SS Doctor Kurt Heissmeyer did tuberculosis testing on prisoners. He had 20 Jewish children sent to him from Auschwitz in Poland. When he was finished experimenting on the children, he had them, and their companions murdered by hanging in the basement of the school at Bullenhuser Damm on the night of April 10, 1944.

Buchenwald

Address: Gedenkstätte Buchenwald
                  D-99427 Weimar, Germany

Phone: 49+36 43 - 430200
Fax: 49+36 43 - 430102

Email: buchenwald@buchenwald.de

WebSite(s):   www.buchenwald.de (in German Only)
            www.scrapbookpages.com/EasternGermany/Buchenwald

Hours: 1st May to 31st Oct   9:45am-6:00pm
                                               (last entry 5:15pm)

                  1st November to 30th April   8:45am-5:00pm
                                               (last entry 4:15pm)

                  CLOSED on MONDAYS.
                  (All "Outdoor" installations are open DAILY until
                  nightfall, but you'd miss many important exhibits if
                  you visit on a Monday when buildings are closed)

Entrance: Free

Schedule: Plan on at least 3 hours to see it all.

Location: Located near WEIMAR & ERFURT area of Germany
                  (northeast of Frankfurt)

Approx Train Travel Time to Weimar:

From: Berlin   6:12
                  Amsterdam   7:47
                  Munich (München)   6:39
                  Hamburg   5:13
                  Nordhausen   1:59

By Train: The nearest train station is Weimar. From there
                  you can either take the bus, taxi, or walk to the camp.

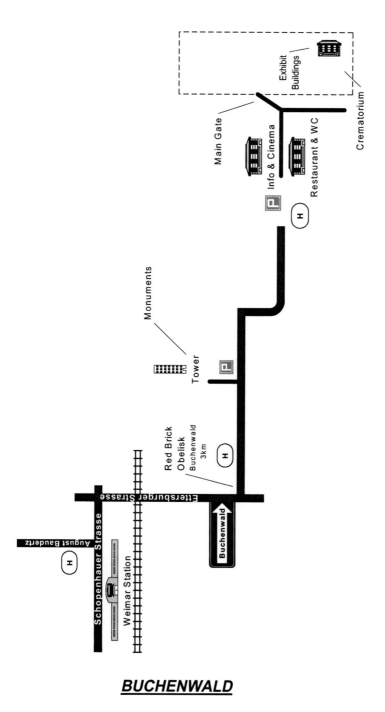

BUCHENWALD

By Bus: Buchenwald lies approx 10km (6¼ miles) north of the city center of Weimar.
City Bus Line #6 leaves daily from Weimar Haupt-bahnhof (train station) Tuesday-Saturday every hour, on the hour 8-6pm (less frequently Sunday) and also from Goetheplatz (opposite the main post office).

Exit the front of the Weimar train station. You will see bus stops across the street. Cross over and turn right and walk a few steps to the corner which is August Baudertplatz and turn left.
You want the bus stop at THAT corner not the ones directly facing the station. Make sure the bus is #6 and that it says Buchenwald (not Ettersburg)
Write down **Gedenkstätte Buchenwald**
to show the driver if unsure. You may pay the bus driver, they make change. Returning from the camp you want the bus going to **Weimar Hauptbahnhof.**
The bus stop at the camp is in the Parking area across from the Gift Shop and Restaurant.

To Walk: **2 Hours.** Exit the front of the Weimar train station and turn Right. You will be on **Schopenhauerstrasse.**
At the end of this street turn Right on **Ettersburger Strasse** and follow this street under the railroad tracks.
After about 20 minutes the sidewalk ends and you'll be walking on grass/gravel along the road.
After 45 minutes to an hour you will reach a fork in the road that is clearly marked.

A red stone obelisk on the Left marks the corner and the signs point the way to the Gedenkstätte 3km (2 miles) down the road to the Left.

About 20 minutes from this corner you will come to a parking area on the Left where there is a very impressive tower & monuments on the hill.
After visiting this area continue in the same direction you were going for about another 15 minutes following the signs to the entrance.

Be sure to pick up an English pamphlet at the Reception/Book Shop.

By Car:
You can take the A4 motorway, Weimar exit, or the B7 Main Road. Once you are on Ettersburger Strasse watch for the signs.

What Remains:
Entrance Gate marked *Jedem Das Seine* (Each To His Own) Crematorium Ovens, foundation ruins of some buildings in the woods, museum buildings with excellent exhibits & disinfection rooms. There is also a small SS Zoo enclosure. The Nazis fed bears right next to the barbed wire in view of starving prisoners.

Camp Opened: July 1937
Date Liberated: April 11, 1945 at 3:15pm by units of the 3rd US Army.

The Clock above the main entrance is purposely STOPPED at 3:15 to mark the exact time the camp was liberated.

95

Mittelbau Dora

Address: Kohnsteinweg 20
D-99734 Nordhausen, Germany

Phone: 49+36+ 313636
Fax: 49+36+ 3140181

Email: info@dora.de
WebPage(s):   www.dora.de   (in German Only)

Hours: April-September Daily 10:00am-6:00pm
October-March Daily 10:00am-4:00pm
Exhibits are Closed on Mondays

Entrance: Free

Schedule: Plan on about 2 hours to see this site.

Location: North of downtown Nordhausen

Approx Train Travel Time to Nordhausen:
From:

Weimar	1:59
Berlin	4:30
Munich (München)	5:50
Hamburg	3:58
Amsterdam	9:21

By Train: Nearest train station is Nordhausen.
From there you can take the small local train called *Harzer Schmalspurbahnen* "HSB" (small fee)
You can buy a ticket at the station, OR pay the driver, they make change.
(Eurailpass is NOT valid on this mini train)
This local mini train has its station right across the street to the Left as you exit the Main train station of Nordhausen. Look for "Nordhausen Nord"
Take this train to the stop <u>Krimderode.</u>

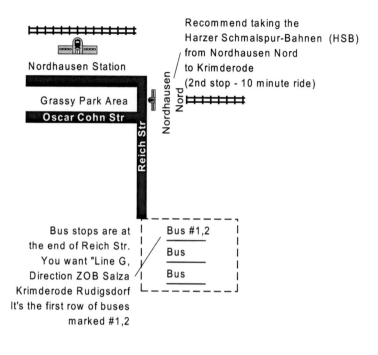

Nordhausen Station

Grassy Park Area

Oscar Cohn Str

Reich Str

Nordhausen Nord

Recommend taking the
Harzer Schmalspur-Bahnen (HSB)
from Nordhausen Nord
to Krimderode
(2nd stop - 10 minute ride)

Bus stops are at
the end of Reich Str.
You want "Line G,
Direction ZOB Salza
Krimderode Rudigsdorf
It's the first row of buses
marked #1,2

Bus #1,2

Bus

Bus

Nordhausen Nord Station **(HSB)** to Krimderode
8:38, 9:21, 10:08, 11:38, 13:08, 14:08 (Daily)

Krimderode to Nordhausen Nord Station **(HSB)**
11:22, 12:22, 13:52, 14:52, 15:52, 16:52 (Daily)

Look for a small white brick shack on the Right.

(They do NOT announce the stops) Krimderode is the 2nd stop approximately 10 minutes from Nordhausen Nord station. From there it is a 15 minute walk to the camp entrance.

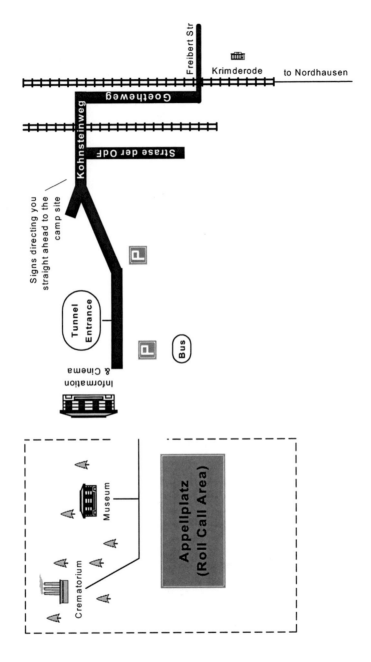

MITTELBAU-DORA

98

To Walk: **15 Minutes.** From Krimderode stop (see map) walk straight ahead down the gravel path in the same direction the train is going. The first street you cross is **Freibert Strasse** which goes to the right. Continue straight ahead down **Goetheweg**. The road curves to the Left becoming **Kohnsteinweg** and crosses over railroad tracks before again curving to the Left.

You will see 2 signs at that 2nd curve directing you straight ahead up the hill. At the fork in the road, keep to the Left into the camp

By Car: Use the B4 to district Nordhausen-Krimderode or the A7 from Hannover taking the Sessen exit.

By Bus: Not Recommended – Very Few Buses Go There.
Exit the front of Nordhausen station. There is a small grassy park directly across the street.
The street goes ahead to the left around this park.
This street is **Reich Strasse**.
You pass Nordhausen Nord station on the left corner (this is where you can take a local train to the camp area). Cross **Oscar-Cohn Strasse** and continue down **Reich Strasse** for about 2 minutes until you reach the line up of bus stops.
You want **Line "G"**
direction: ZOB Salza Krimderode Rüdigsdorf
It is the First Row (Stops 1,2)
Bus service is NOT frequent.

> Nordhausen Bus Station to Mittelbau Dora
>   9:15, 11:45, 13:45   (Mon-Fri only)
>
> Mittelbau Dora to Nordhausen Bus Station
>   12:24, 17:24 (Mon-Fri only)

What Remains:
Museum with exhibits in German.
Ask for an English translation guide book to use (& return) while walking through the museum. Films, artifacts, crematorium, foundations of buildings. Follow the paths through the woods to see some ruins.
Some markers along the walkways have descriptions in English.

Crematorium Building in the woods

Not to be missed are the Tunnels (shown by Tour Guide Only)

To hide armament factories the prisoners had to carve out these tunnels & were forced to build V2 rockets inside the mountain.

English Tours are usually at 11:00 & 14:00 Tues. through Fri. Check at the information office (a few people speak English there) to confirm tour times.

There is a Cinema with an excellent 25 minute film to show you what you are about to see. This film can be viewed at anytime. Just ask, and as long as a Group is not waiting to view it in another language, they will turn on the English version of the film for you.

Camp Opened: August 1943 as a subcamp of Buchenwald. In October 1944 it became an independent camp.

Date Liberated: April 11, 1945 by US soldiers

Gardelegen

Address: Mahn und Gedenkstätte Gardelegen
Office In Town Rathausplatz 10
39638 Gardelegen, Germany

Phone: 49+ 03907 / 6519
Fax: 49+ 03907 / 6586

Email: None Available
WebSite(s): www.geocities.com/Pentagon/7087/uk076.htm
www.102ndinfantrydivision.homestead.com/Gardelegen1.html

Hours: Offices in town are open Mon-Fri 8am-4pm or by appointment. The site with the memorial wall and grave can be viewed at any time.

Entrance: Free

Schedule: Plan on about 15 minutes to view this site.

Location: Outskirts of Gardelegen which is midway between Berlin and Hamburg and approximately 30km (18½ miles) north of Magdeburg.

Approx Train Travel Time to Gardelegen:
From: Berlin 3:02
Hamburg 2:40
Nordhausen 3:58

By Train: Gardelegen station is the closest.

By Bus: There is a bus stop directly in front of the Gardelegen train station. Buses run approximately every hour in the direction of Bismarker Str. The closest bus STOP to the memorial that I could find was on Bismarker Strasse about a 2 minute walk to the round-a-bout at Isenschnibber Chausse/Gilforner Strasse. (see map "H" is bus stop).

As always, write down where you wish to go
Mahn und Gedenkstätte Gardelegen
and show the driver. The bus just MIGHT continue
closer although there is no bus stop near the turn off
for the memorial that I could see.

By Car: Take the B71 or B188
to Gardelegen,
Bismarker Strasse.
The memorial is just
off the round-a-bout at
the intersection of
Bismarker Str,
Isenschnibber Chausse
& Gilforner Str.
Look for this sign

Monument and Memorial

To Walk: **45 Minutes.** Exit the front of Gardelegen train station
and turn Left. You will be on Bahnhofstrasse. When
you reach the intersection where it splits turn Right.
You will be on Hopfenstrasse which changes names to
Ernst Thalman Strasse further down. A few blocks
down you will come to the corner of Schiller Strasse
(Postamt Office on the left). Turn Right down
Schiller Strasse & walk for about eight minutes. This
street will curve to the left and end up at the intersection of Stendaler Strasse where you turn Right. At the
Round-a-Bout you want to cross the street to the Left
and walk down Bismarker Strasse (Stay on the Right
side of Bismarker Str) About a 13 minute walk down
Bismarker Str. you come to another Round-a-Bout.
Isenschnibber Chausse goes to the left and Gilforner
Strasse to the right. You want to go straight ahead on
the other side of the round-a-bout. You see a building
marked "Hastra" on the left corner and behind it a tall
radio tower. You'll see a big sign on the Right side of
the road a block down **"Mahn und Gedenkstätte"**
directing you to the Right down Am Kammereiforst.
It's a 13 minute walk from this point down a country
road of empty land & cornfields. At the end you can
only turn Left. Walk a few minutes past the high trees
and you'll see the memorial in the middle of nowhere.

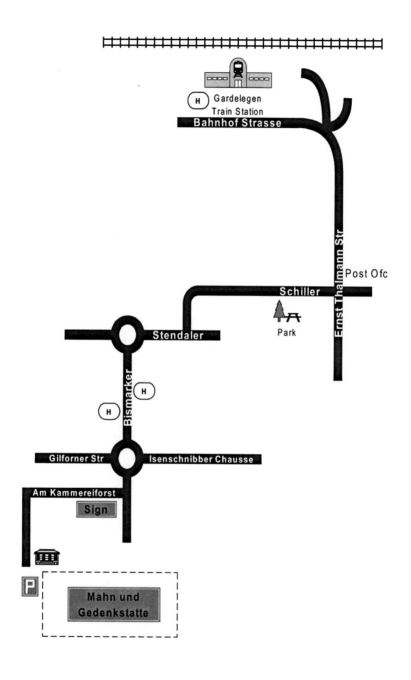

Gardelegen Train Station

Bahnhof Strasse

Ernst Thalmann Str

Post Ofc

Schiller

Park

Stendaler

Bismarcker

Gilforner Str

Isenschnibber Chausse

Am Kammereiforst

Sign

P

Mahn und Gedenkstatte

GARDELEGEN

What Remains: Monuments, part of the barn & a cemetery.

Background: Gardelegen was not a Concentration Camp.
During WWII it was used as an army base and training facility for parachutists. During the month of April 1945 Gardelegen was one of the final destinations of the "Death Marches"
(When Allied Troops were getting too close to the various camps, such as Neuengamme, the Nazi's forced inmates to walk in the direction of other sites. Many died along the way).
On April 13, 1945, 1016 concentration camp prisoners were locked inside a barn in the Isenschnibbe field and burned alive.
The very next day American Troops arrived and found the bodies still smoldering in the rubble.

Gardelegen Memorial

Remaining facade of the barn

Flossenbürg

Address: KZ-Grab-und Gedenkstätte Flossenbürg
Gedächtnisallee 7
92696 Flossenbürg, Germany

Phone: 49+9603 / 921980
Fax: 49+9603 / 921990

E-Mail: information@gedenkstaette-flossenbuerg.de
Webpage(s):   www.thirdreichruins.com/flossenburg.htm
www.gedenkstaette-flossenbuerg.de
(in German only)

Hours: Daily 9am-5pm

Entrance: Free

Schedule: Plan on about 2½ hours to visit and view the film.

Location: Camp Site is Northeast of Weiden, Germany.

Approx Train Travel Time to Weiden:
From:

Nürnberg	1:03
Munich (München)	2:38
Weimar	6:08
Nordhausen	5:30
Berlin	6:00

By Train: Nearest Train station is Weiden.

By Bus: Approx 1 Hour ride from the bus stop outside Weiden
Train Station. Mon-Fri buses leave about every 2
hours; Sat-Sun/Holidays less frequent
You may pay the driver, they make change.

BUS SCHEDULE:
Weiden BF to Flossenbürg/Gedenkstätte
7:30, 10:20, 12:35 etc

Flossenbürg/Gedenkstätte to Weiden BF
11:23, 13:40, 15:20 etc

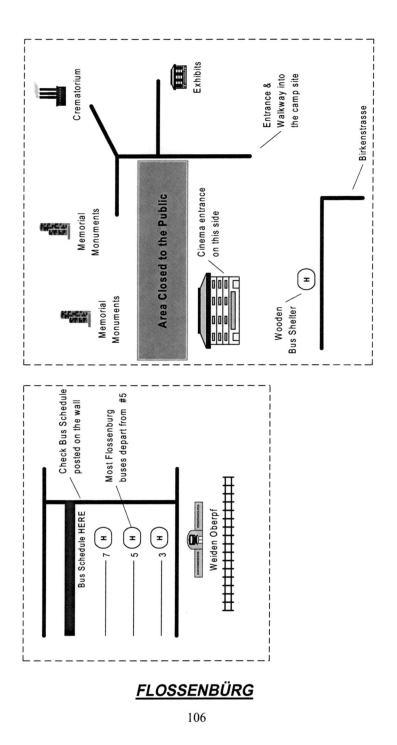

FLOSSENBÜRG

Walk out the front of the Weiden train station and you'll see the Bus stops directly across the street. There are rows of stops marked with an "**H**" (denotes Bus stops in Germany). Most of the Flossenbürg/Gedenkstätte buses are lined up at **#5.** (Check the Schedule located on a Board behind the last row of buses).

NOTE: There are (4) Flossenbürg Bus stops. You want the 4th Stop which is at the Gedenkstätte (Memorial) Likewise, Weiden has Many Bus stops. You want the one that says "WEIDEN BF" (Bahnhof or Train Station).

They do NOT announce the stops along the way. How will you know which stop is yours? You need to watch out the window for signs. Approximately 40 minutes into the ride when you enter the town of Flossenbürg be looking for signs.

(KZ Flossenbürg)
The camp site will be coming up shortly. It will be on the Right side of the bus. The bus makes a left turn and stops at a wide open area with a big brick building and a small wooden bus enclosure (circled below).

107

Press the RED Button by the rear door or on the Rail above the front seat behind the driver to signal that you want to get off at this stop.

(as always, it's best to Write Down where you are going "**KZ Flossenbürg**", show it to the driver and try to sit in the front right seat. Most drivers are helpful and will motion to you, when it's your stop if they know you aren't sure). The camp entrance is behind and to the Right of the big brick building, which houses the cinema showing a short film (free) on the history of this place. (there is a small dress shop right next to the entrance to the camp).

What Remains:

Small museum building with a few exhibits. Foundation of several buildings, a crematorium building with oven & dissection room. Guard tower, memorial pyramid of ashes.

Pyramid of ashes near the crematorium

Camp Opened:	First transport of foreign prisoners arrived April 5, 1940, although the camp was used starting in 1938 as a prison.
Date Liberated:	April 23, 1945 by the Americans

MUNICH (München) area

Approx Train Travel Time to Munich (München Hbf):
From: Berlin 8:12
Amsterdam 10:34
Linz (Austria) 3:15
Nürnberg (Nuremberg) 1:40
Strasbourg 4:52

Munich S-Bahn & U-Bahn:
www.reed.edu/~reyn/munich2002.jpg

(Third Reich Sites) I recommend the *"MUNICH WALKS"* tours.

The tours are very informative and an inexpensive way to see the city and ask questions. They meet in the Munich Hauptbahnhof (main rail station) outside the EurAide office by Track 11.

The tour covers many interesting buildings relating to the Nazi period, among them, the Feldherrnhalle, site of the 1923 Beer Hall Putsch.

These tours run daily from April 1st to October 31st.
For more information on exact days & times check website or pick up a brochure at the EurAide office by Track 11 in Munich Hauptbahnhof.
(No prior booking is required to take the tours, just show up)

WebSite: www.munichwalks.com
E-Mail: info@radiusmunich.com
Phone: 49+89 55 02 93 74
Fax: 49+89 59 47 14

Dachau

Address: Alte Romerstrasse 75
                   D-85221 Dachau, Germany

Phone: 49+ 8131 669970
Fax: 49+ 8131 2235

E-mail: info@kz-gedenkstaette-dachau.de
Webpage: www.kz-gedenkstaette-dachau.de/english/index.html

Hours: Tuesday-Sunday 9am-5pm
                  CLOSED on MONDAYS

Entrance: Free

Schedule: Plan on about 2 hours to see this site.
                  4 Hours if you take the Free Guided Tour.

Location: Dachau is approximately 20 minutes by train
                  northwest of Munchen (Munich)

Munich S-Bahn & U-Bahn:
                  www.reed.edu/~reyn/munich2002.jpg

By S-Bahn: From München (Munich) Hbf take the **S2** in the
direction of Dachau or Peterhausen. S-Bahn tracks are
located downstairs at the train station. As you exit the
regular trains, turn Left and the stairs down are at the
end of the station.
*Note: Eurailpasses are Valid on S-Bahn trains,
       but not U-Bahn.*
*If you don't have a pass and need to purchase an
S-Bahn ticket there are machines in the station.*
Exit at Dachau station (about 7 stops, 30 minutes from
München) From there take the bus or walk.

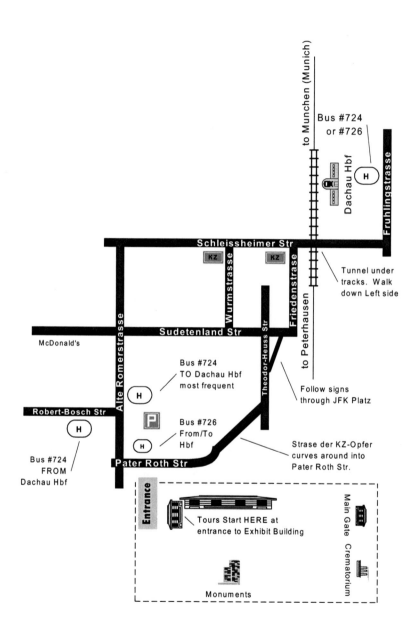

DACHAU

By Bus: When you exit the S-Bahn train you will go downstairs and then Left out to the street. Out front of Dachau station is the bus stop. **#724** & **#726** both go to the Gedenkstätte (Memorial) These 2 buses stop at different corners, both only steps from the camp. (See map) **#724** runs more frequently than #726 You may pay the driver, they make change. Punch your ticket in the Red Box on the bus to validate it.

BUS SCHEDULE:
Dachau Station to Gedenkstätte Dachau
8:07, 8:27, 8:47, 9:07, 9:27, 9:47 etc

Gedenkstätte Dachau to Dachau Station
9:12, 9:32, 9:52, 10:12, 10:32, 10:52 etc

To Walk:
45 Minutes. (Mostly residential area) Exit Dachau station and turn Right. You'll be on Fruhlingstrasse. It's a 3 minute walk to the next intersection where you will cross the street and turn Right down Schleissheimer Strasse (under the tracks) . The next corner will be Friedenstrasse and a sign directing you to go Left. You have a choice. You can either turn Left and follow the signs to Sudetenland Str, about 15 minutes, then cross over and follow signs that mark the path through JFK Platz where it crosses Theodor-Heuss Str., keeping to the Right on Strase der KZ-Opfer  which turns into Pater Roth Str. ending up at the camp.

    OR (and this way is less confusing if you ask me) instead of turning left back on Friedenstrasse, continue straight ahead down Schleissheimer Str. About 20 minutes down you will come to the corner of Würmstrasse (look for a very small sign on the corner that says "Concentration Camp Memorial" pointing Left.
Turn Left down Würmstrasse and go to the end, about 6 minutes to Sudetenland Strasse and turn Right.
The next major intersection is Alte Romerstrasse. Turn Left and the camp will be about 5 minutes down Alte Romerstrasse on the Left (there are NO signs at this corner directing you to the camp)

What Remains:
Museum building with some very good exhibits.

Cinema, reconstructed barracks, original gate with the familiar
"Arbeit Macht Frei" (work makes freedom)

Crematorium

Shower room (not used to gas anyone)
also disinfection chambers for clothes,
and several monuments.

FREE GUIDED TOUR
(Approximately 2½ Hours)

I highly recommend this _**Excellent**_ tour. It gives you an
incredible amount of information, not only about Dachau, but about the
Holocaust in general. I found it well worth the time.

Free Tours in **English** meet at the Museum Entrance
at 1:30 Tuesday through Friday
Saturdays and Sundays at 12:00 and 1:30

Camp Opened: March 1933
Date Liberated: April 29, 1945

Background: Dachau was the First concentration camp.

Hadamar (Euthanasia Site)

Address: Gedenkstätte Hadamar
Mönchberg 8
65589 Hadamar Germany

Phone: 49+ 64 33 917- 174
Fax: 49+ 64 33 917- 175

E-mail: None Available
Webpage: www.deathcamps.org/t4/hadamar.html

Hours: Open ONLY Tuesday, Wednesday & Thursdays 9-4
and Every First Sunday in the month 11-4pm
(except holidays) (Closed Dec 22 - Jan 1st)

Entrance: Free

Schedule: Plan on about 1 hour to view this site.

Location: Hadamar is a small town located not far from
Limburg, Germany

Approx Train Travel Time to Hadamar (via Limburg):

From:	
Berlin	7:23
Amsterdam	5:58
Munich (München)	5:40
Hamburg	5:45

By Train: The nearest big city is Koblenz where you can get a
train to Limburg (approx 1 hour) and then connect to
Hadamar (approx 20 minutes)
(Do NOT get off at Niederhadamar, HADAMAR is
the Next stop)

To Walk:

5 Minutes. The Hadamar station (closed & locked)
is a yellow dilapidated old structure. No lockers or facilities. Standing
by the tracks, with the station on your Right, look down the tracks and
then up to the Left on the
hill. You'll see a Church.
The Hadamar Institute is
Behind that Church.
Walk behind the station
building & turn Left,
you'll be on AM Bahnhof.
Take the 2nd street that
goes left, this is Brücken-
vorstadt. It goes under the
railroad tracks and curves

uphill. When it forks, keep to the Right up Mönchberg Strasse (the
street sign is on the corner building but hidden by a tree). Halfway up
the hill (behind the church on the right) is the Hadamar Institute. You
will be going into the yellowish colored Main Building. The entrance to
the Gedenkstätte (Memorial) is on the Right side of the building.

By Car: Highway A48 (direction Frankfurt)
Highway A3 (direction Frankfurt) exit "Limburg Nord"
Road B49/B54 (direction "Siegen/Geisen") 3rd exit Road
B54 (direction "Siegen") 1st exit "Hadamar"
Once in Hadamar, follow the signs to:
"Gedenkstätte Mönchberg" / "Psych. Krankenhaus"

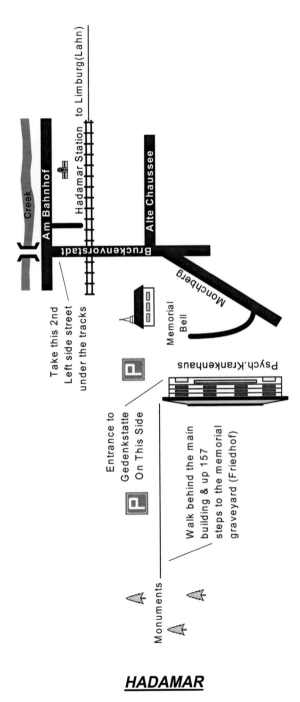

Creek

Am Bahnhof

Hadamar Station to Limburg(Lahn)

Bruckenvorstadt

Alte Chaussee

Monchberg

Take this 2nd
Left side street
under the tracks

Memorial
Bell

Psych.Krankenhaus

Entrance to
Gedenkstatte
On This Side

Walk behind the main
building & up 157
steps to the memorial
graveyard (Friedhof)

Monuments

HADAMAR

What Remains:

It is still used as a medical facility to this day. The bottom floor has several rooms dedicated to what happened here. All exhibits are in German Only. Pick up a free English brochure that explains the site. The Basement has the gas chamber room, a dissection table, a "picture" of the crematorium (all mechanical devices were dismantled by the Nazis) and not much more.

Gas Chamber

Out Back of the building and up a steep 157 steps is the Friedhof (graveyard) with a few monuments.

Background:

Not only did the Nazis have concentration "Death Camps" but they also enlisted Hospitals and other sites to perform what they deemed necessary for the good of the Third Reich. The ' Euthanasie' System was used to murder what they called "USELESS EATERS" This could be the Mentally Ill, Alcoholics, Retarded, Dimwitted, Half-Jewish inmates of remand homes, Tuberculosis Patients, to name a few. They would be taken by bus to special gas-chamber institutions set up in sanitariums or hospitals.

The 6 Institutions of which Hadamar was the last one:

Grafeneck	(9839 victims)	**Brandenburg**	(9772 victims)
Bernburg	(8601 victims)	**Hadamar**	(10,072 victims)
Hartheim	(18,269 victims)	**Sonnenstein**	(13,720 victims)

During January-August 1941 more than 10,000 men, women & children were murdered with monoxide gas in chambers disguised as showers at the Hadamar facility. After the Euthanasia policy was ended in August of 1941, the gas chambers were dismantled, but the killing continued. Doctors and nurses would murder patients with overdoses of medication, or leave them to starve to death, so the numbers in parenthesis above only estimate the gassings, not the murders that occurred after the gas-chambers were dismantled.

Nürnberg Courthouse   (Nuremberg)

Address: Justizbehörden
Fürther Strasse 110
90429 Nürnberg, Germany

Phone: 49+911-3212607
Fax: 49+911-3212233

Email: None Available
Webpage:
http://fcit.coedu.usf.edu/holocaust/resource/gallery/n1945.htm
www.mtsu.edu/%7Ebaustin/trials3.html

Hours: Room **#600** (located upstairs in the smaller building
to the right and behind the larger main building at
#110) is still used as a court for major trials today.
It is NOT a Museum.
Visitors may visit Room #600 by applying in advance
to the above address indicating your arrival date and
time. This is *recommended*, and by doing so you stand
a better chance of having a guide available to you.
You CAN just show up and go to the guard at the
smaller building or the main building and simply ask
"May I please visit Room #600"
They will do their best to accommodate you, but there
is no guarantee.
If there are no trials in session you may take pictures.
If there IS a trial in session, visitors are usually
allowed in to watch, but no pictures may be taken at
that time. Usually there are court sessions on
Tuesdays and Thursdays.

Approx Train Travel Time to Nürnberg:
From: Munich (München)   1:40
Berlin   7:52
Amsterdam   9:38

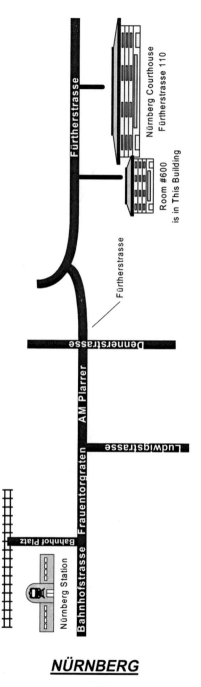

NÜRNBERG

To Walk: <u>**50 Minutes.**</u> Exit the front of the Nürnberg train station & turn Left. You'll be on Bahnhofstrasse. Walk to the Left you cross Bahnhofplatz. At the corner cross over to the other side of Bahnhofstrasse and continue walking left, away from the train station. The street is now called Frauentorgraben. Continue ahead until you come to a grassy divider in the middle of the street where you will keep to the Right crossing Ludwigstrasse. The street again splits off to the Right with a building in the middle. This time cross the street (Spittlertorgraben) and walk to the Left of that building down Am Plärrer. When you reach the next main intersection where cars can only go to the left, cross that street (Dennerstrasse) and continue straight ahead down Fürther Strasse. The street merges with Sudliche Fürther Strasse. Continue walking to the Right. You are now on the street where the courthouse is located at **#110** It will be on the Right approximately 15 minutes walking time from this point.

When you reach the massive courthouse at 110 Fürther Strasse you can either enter through the front of the Main Building and see the guard at the desk or go directly to the smaller building located to the Right and slightly in Back of the larger main building to see the guard there.

This smaller building is where Room #600 is located upstairs.

120

By U-Bahn: Go downstairs inside the front of the train station and there you will find the U-Bahn. You can buy a ticket from the machines. You want to go in the direction of Furth getting off at the Barenschanze stop. When you exit at Barenschanze go up to ground level & continue in the same direction the train was going. (you'll be on Fürther Strasse). You should be walking down the Right Side of Fürther Strasse looking for the courthouse at #110. When returning by U-Bahn your destination will be the Hauptbahnhof (Main Train Station).

What Remains:

It is a working courtroom. The furniture is NOT the original from the trial days. If you have a guide they will explain about the passageways behind the area where Göring & Hess and the others sat and

give you more information. It is best to read up on the trial before visiting in case you do not get a guide. There is also a wall with some information downstairs by the entrance to this smaller building. Ask for an English pamphlet for useful information.

Background: The Site of the Nuremberg War Trials for Crimes Against Humanity.

Recommended Viewing:

Judgment at Nuremberg (1961)
Spencer Tracy 178 minutes
Loosely based on actual events but still gives you a sense of the drama that unfolded in this room.

Nuremberg (2000) made for TV
Alec Baldwin 179 minutes

Eagle's Nest/Berchtesgaden (Hitler's Mountaintop Retreat)

Address: Visitors Center Berchtesgadener Land
For info only   Konigsseerstr. 2
                 83471 Berchtesgaden
                 Germany

Phone: 49+ 86+ 52 967 102
                 49+ 86+ 52 29 69   (Kehlsteinhaus/Eagles Nest)
Fax: 49+ 86+ 52 6 33 00

Email: info@Berchtesgaden.de   (Tourist Information)
                 berchtesgaden@rvo-bus.de   (Bus information)

Webpage(s):
        www.berchtesgadener-land.com
        www.scrapbookpages.com/Kehlsteinhaus/index.html

Hours: The House (now a Restaurant) is open from Mid May
until the end of October (depending on the weather,
if heavy snows, it closes earlier)
Suggest E-Mailing the above E-mail addresses if your
travel plans call for a visit in Early May or Late
October to be sure it's open.

Entrance: Small Fee to take the elevator to the top, but if
you came by bus, it's Included with your bus ticket.

Schedule: Plan on about 30 minutes at the top, 1 hour if you are
taking the 30 minute guided tour.
Then another hour at the base (Hintereck) to visit the
air raid bunkers and surrounding area.

Location: In Germany approximately one hour train ride
southwest of Salzburg, Austria.

Approx Train Travel Time to Berchtesgaden:
From:

From:	
Salzburg	1:00
Munich (München)	2:45
Berlin	10:00
Amsterdam	12:00

By Bus: Exit the front of Berchtesgaden train station and turn Right. Walk down to the end and look for **"RVO Fahrschein Vorverkauf"** In this office buy a Roundtrip Bus ticket to the *KEHLSTEINHAUS* (Eagle's Nest is a name given to this place because of its location) (approx. $15 US) includes entrance. Approximately 35 minute ride with buses running about every half hour. You may pay the driver, they make change, but I suggest buying your ticket at the bus office.

The person in the office spoke some English, the driver did not.

It will be **Bus Stop #1** which is directly out the door from the ticket window. Sign Says *"Oberau-Rosfeld, Obersalzberg-Kehlstein"*

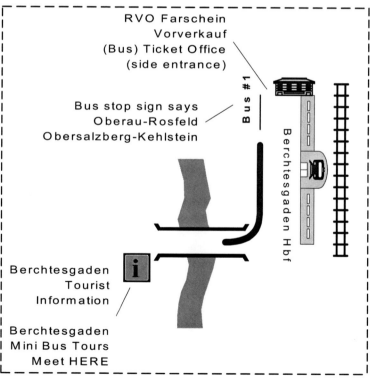

Try to Sit on the RIGHT SIDE of the bus on the Way Up! Trust Me!!

Some of the buses go all the way to the top, some require a change of bus at the base of the mountain (Hintereck) where there is a small gift shop, tour office and restaurant. If everyone gets off the bus at Hintereck then you need to change buses. If not, the bus will proceed to the top in about 5 minutes. Either way it's easy to reach.

Nothing will say *"Eagles Nest"* until you get to Hintereck.
It is actually called the "Kehlsteinhaus" (house on the Kehlstein mountain)

At the bus stop at the base of the hill (Hintereck) you can spend some time upon your return touring the Air Raid Shelter tunnels located a short walk down the hill to the Left of the bus stop. From Hintereck to the top a "Recorded" explanation is given in German, then English about what you are seeing.

This heart-stopping ride to the top is very scenic, with hair-pin turns, sheer drop-offs on cliffhanging roads.

Get your Cameras Ready!

IMPORTANT:

Reserve your spot on the return bus when you arrive. There is a ticket window to the right of the tunnel to the elevator. Tell them what time you want to return from the times shown on the wall. They will stamp your ticket with your return time. (1½ hours is plenty of time to visit) Your Bus Ticket gains you entry into the elevator to the top.

If you are Not taking a tour, simply go up on your own when ready. When returning, again you might get a bus all the way to the Bahnhof or you might have to change in Hintereck. But I suggest getting off in Hintereck either way so you can visit the Air Raid Bunkers. (see map) Buses BACK to the Berchtesgaden train station line up at **Stop #7** marked Berchtesgaden Bahnhof. Your Roundtrip ticket is good for the entire trip, including this stopover.

Be sure to hold on to your ticket for the return!

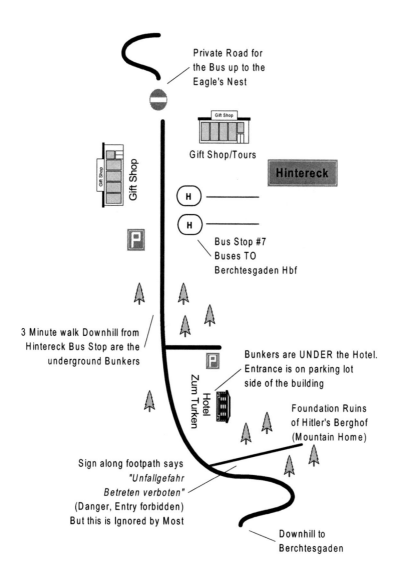

Private Road for the Bus up to the Eagle's Nest

Gift Shop/Tours

Gift Shop

Gift Shop

Hintereck

Bus Stop #7
Buses TO
Berchtesgaden Hbf

3 Minute walk Downhill from Hintereck Bus Stop are the underground Bunkers

Hotel Zum Turken

Bunkers are UNDER the Hotel. Entrance is on parking lot side of the building

Foundation Ruins of Hitler's Berghof (Mountain Home)

Sign along footpath says
"Unfallgefahr Betreten verboten"
(Danger, Entry forbidden)
But this is Ignored by Most

Downhill to Berchtesgaden

EAGLE'S NEST

Tunnel entrance to Elevator for ride to the House above

What Remains:
THE EAGLE'S NEST: (Kehlsteinhaus)
The house is now a restaurant. No mention of Hitler can be found.
There are no signs, exhibits, pictures, NOTHING!
It is best to take a Tour, or read up beforehand or you will be somewhat disappointed by your visit when all you see is a dining room. The View (on a clear day when you are not surrounded by clouds) is *__Incredible!__* You may have seen the old films of Hitler with Eva Braun standing on the balcony of this house. You can walk up the hill behind to a cross on the hilltop and do some hiking if you like. (Be Careful, VERY Rocky)

Up in the clouds at the Eagle's Nest

The house is now only a restaurant. This is one of the dining rooms.

Tours: A very informative 25 minute English tour (small fee) is available Daily at 10:30 and 11:40. It meets near the elevator to the top. The guide usually stands outside nearby the ticket window where you reserve your time back down the hill. No Reservation Required.

If time allows and you plan IN ADVANCE of arriving at the top, the same company offers longer tours of the entire area. They offer a 4-hour tour (limited to 8 persons) leaving at 1:30 daily (mid May through October) from the tourist office located opposite the Berchtesgaden train station. Exiting Berchtesgaden station look across the street, slightly to the left across the bridge you will see "INFORMATION" written on a building. This is the Tourist Office. This tour gives you an extensive look at the area, the history, the trip to the Eagle's Nest & the Bunker System along with an explanation of about 40 remaining buildings of that period. They offer free hotel pick-ups in Berchtesgaden.

BERCHTESGADEN MINI BUS TOURS
49+ 86+ 52 64971   or fax 49+ 86+ 52 64863
E-mail: info@eagles-nest-tours.com

AIR RAID BUNKERS
Website: www.hotel-zum-tuerken.com
Located under the Hotel Zum Turken (former SS Headquarters)

Back at the base stop "Hintereck" it's a 3 minute walk down the road to the Left of the buses. You will see the hotel on the Left.
The entrance to the tunnels is a door on the side of the hotel facing the parking lot.

OPEN: DAILY 9am-3pm
          Nov. 1 to Dec 15 and Jan. 10 to Mar. 31
          DAILY 7am-6pm all other dates.

NOTE:
It is an Automatic Turnstile which only accepts coins to enter.
The day I was there, nobody was around the small snack window to make change and over 20 tourists had to walk away without seeing it because none of them had **coins** in their pockets!

In the bunker, which goes deep underground are hallways, stairways leading to small rooms. This was where the SS planned to hide in the event of air raids.

HITLER'S BERG HOF (mountain house)

A few steps further
down the hill from the
Hotel Zum Turken is
a dirt path leading
into the woods.

It is marked with a sign.....

Unfallgefahr
Betreten verboten
(Danger, Entry forbidden)

....but this is mostly ignored.

Nothing remains of Hitler's house in the woods except the ruins of
the foundation retaining walls which are now overgrown with weeds
& trees. It was destroyed & completely demolished to keep it from
becoming a shrine to Hitler.

Background: Hitler never lived in the Eagle's Nest house.
He used it to impress his guests.
He preferred the Berg Hof (Mountain House)
located down the hill.

AUSTRIA (Österreich)

Mauthausen

Address: KZ-Gedenkstätte Mauthausen
Erinnerungsstrasse 1
A-4310 Mauthausen, Austria

Phone(s): 43+ 7238 2269 0
43+ 7238 2269 8 (Info)
43+ 7238 2269 9 (Book shop)

Fax: 43+ 7238 2269 40

E-mail: mauthausen-memorial@mail.bmi.gv.at

WebSite(s): www.mauthausen-memorial.at
http://remember.org/camps/mauthausen/mau-list.html
www.nizkor.org/hweb/camps/gusen/gugas01x.htm

Hours: 1 Feb - 31 Mar, and 1 Oct - 15 Dec
Daily 8:00am - 4:00pm (last entry 3:00 pm)
1 Apr - 30 Sep
Daily 8:00am - 6:00pm (last entry 5:00 pm)
The camp site is closed 16 Dec through 31 Jan

Entrance: Small Fee

Schedule: Plan on at least 3 hours to see this site.

Location: Short distance east of Linz, Austria.
An easy 2 hour train West of Vienna "Wien".
You could do an "Out and Back" day trip from
Vienna to Mauthausen. If coming from Vienna take a
train to St. Valentin and change for Mauthausen.

Approx Train Travel Time to Linz:

From:		
Vienna (Wien)	1:47
Salzburg	1:21
Munich (München)	3:15
Krakow	12:17
Prague (Praha)	6:13

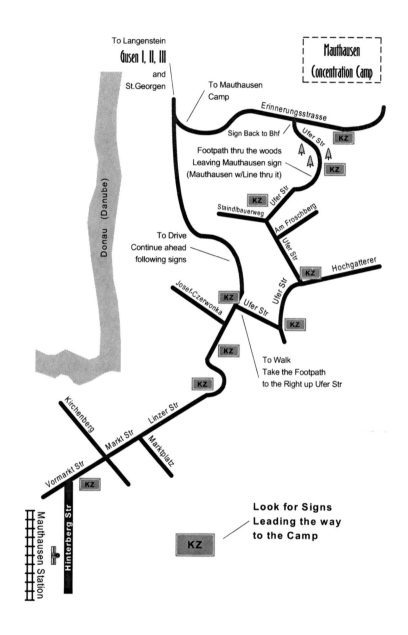

MAUTHAUSEN

131

By Car: Take the B3 Highway from Linz toward
                 Mauthausen. Follow the signs leading from the B3 to
                 Linzerstrasse and up the hill to the camp.

By Train: From Linz you must change trains in St Valentin:
                 Linz to St Valentin (approx 15 minutes)
                 St Valentin to Mauthausen (approx 7 minutes)

By Taxi: From Mauthausen call Brixner Taxi Co. Phone 2439
                 (07238 2439 from other Austrian cities)

To Walk:

1 Hour. There are two routes. One goes on the backside of the hills and the other through town. I suggest going through town, it's more interesting! Upon leaving the train, you will be walking to the LEFT down Hinterberg Strasse the street that runs Behind the station. There are MANY signs from the train station leading the way to the camp. Look for this:

Ehem. KZ Mauthausen ("Ehem" means Former)

A few steps down Hinterberg Strasse the road becomes Vormarktstrasse (notice on many buildings, the street NAME is shown along with the #) The street will change names several times, but continue straight ahead following the very visible signs. You will see a sign pointing to the Left towards the River. This is the route for cars. If walking, continue ahead. After crossing Kirchenberg the street becomes Marktstrasse, after passing Marktplatz it becomes Linzerstr. After about 15-20 minutes you will come to a corner marked Josef-Czerwenka to the Left and Ufer-Strasse to the Right. There is a store on the Right side and on the Left side a sign that says **Footpath to the Former Concentration Camp**

If *Walking* turn RIGHT up Ufer Strasse 2km – 1¼ mi. If *Driving* continue straight ahead on Linzerstrasse following signs up the hill to the parking area. Ufer Strasse is a residential street (not really a path) that twists and turns its way up the hill to the camp. Follow the signs which lead you gradually uphill to the Left.

When you see a sign that says Mauthausen with a line through it *(don't be confused into thinking it means Mauthausen Camp is not this way, it Means you are Leaving the Town of Mauthausen)* you will then be on a gravel footpath through a wooded area. To reach the camp entrance at the top of the hill, turn Right on Erinnerungsstrasse and continue uphill past the bus parking lot and the swimming pool the Nazis had built.

There is a **Visitors Center** on the right as you face the camp. Inside is the book shop and videos of survivors giving their testimonies. You can listen via headphones.

Mauthausen is a HUGE Fortress

You enter a small door and walk through a courtyard and then upstairs and turn Right.
The Ticket Window is by the entrance upstairs.

After visiting the inside of the camp, walk back out past the ticket window & straight ahead to see several monuments on the grounds.

Continue ahead & you'll see a sign leading you to the Todesstiege. (The Death Staircase). This is the 186 Steps that the prisoners had to walk up and down carrying boulders from the quarry.

Camp Opened: August 8, 1938
Date Liberated: May 5, 1945

What Remains:
Gas Chamber was not destroyed. You can walk in, close the door and look through the peep hole used by the Nazis to watch their victims suffocating. Crematorium ovens, sezierraum (dissection room) & refrigeration room to store the bodies. Museum with exhibits. Barrack buildings. Bookstore. Swimming pool used by the Nazis to relax after a hard days work. Death Staircase (186 Steps) to the quarry below. Memorial Monuments.

Entrance to the Gas Chamber

Peep Hole in the door. The Nazis watched as their victims suffocated inside.

Crematorium

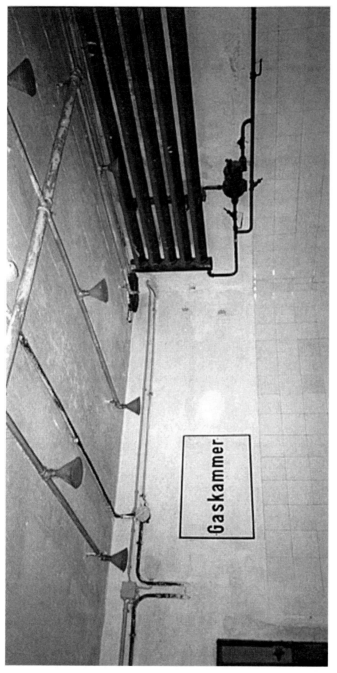

The Gas Chamber at Mauthausen was not destroyed
It's a chilling reminder of the atrocities that happened here

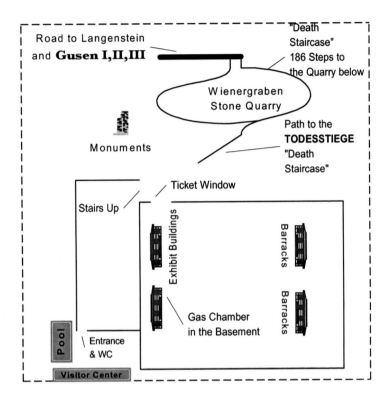

Road to Langenstein and **Gusen I,II,III**

"Death Staircase" 186 Steps to the Quarry below

Wienergraben Stone Quarry

Path to the **TODESSTIEGE** "Death Staircase"

Monuments

Ticket Window

Stairs Up

Exhibit Buildings

Barracks

Barracks

Gas Chamber in the Basement

Pool

Entrance & WC

Visitor Center

Zyklon B Gas Can

Once the pellets hit the air they vaporized killing the victims in about 15 minutes.

MAUTHAUSEN CAMP

Gusen I, II, III (Adjacent to Mauthausen)

Address: Martha Gammer
(for info)   Sperlhang 4
          A-4222 St.Georgen/Gusen, Austria

Phone: +43 7237 3946
Fax: +43 7229 76920

E-mail(s):   hannes.gammer@vpn.at
          erhd@nextra.at

WebSite(s):   www.gusen.org
          www.nizkor.org/hweb/camps/gusen/gugas01x.htm

Hours: Not a Museum so you may drive or walk around
          this area at any time.
          Write to the Above Address or E-Mail for more
          information. A guide can sometimes be arranged for
          groups or individuals wishing to be shown around
          this area. **Without guidance this area would be**
          difficult to understand and visualize.

Schedule: With a guide, plan on about 2 Hours to drive around
          and have the major buildings that are left pointed
          out to you. (None are open to the public)

Approx Train Travel Time to St Georgen a d Gusen
From: Linz   0:18 minutes

NOTE:
This site has become one of the so-called "Forgotten" Camps.
It was larger than Mauthausen Main Camp and worked along side
Mauthausen in day-to-day operations of the stone quarries.
Gusen I, II, III is VERY spread out over a large area. Unlike the
"Show Camps" of Mauthausen and Auschwitz which are pretty much
confined to a walled-in area, Gusen has become part of the local
residential scene.
Homes and businesses have been built on the site. Many of the
original buildings are now private residences of the citizens of this
area. You cannot visit these buildings and there are few markers
denoting what it is that you are seeing.

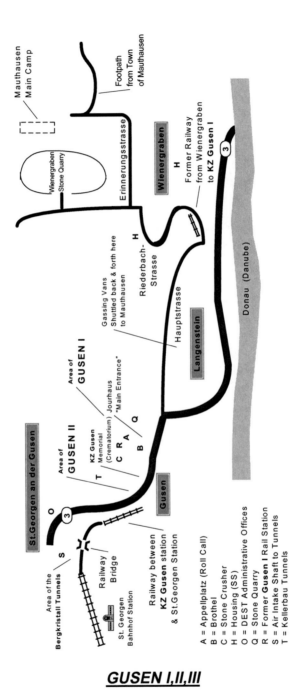

GUSEN I,II,III

Private citizens have organized to try and preserve what little is left, but as of this writing, new homes are being built on top of the tunnel shafts. Most of the area from the Death Staircase at Mauthausen Main Camp, down the road to the left all the way through Langenstein to St Georgen a d Gusen was part of Gusen territory.

Today, as you drive or walk through this part of the countryside you would have no idea what you are looking at.

What Remains:

Main Entrance (now a private residence), Air ventilation shaft from armament factory tunnels built in the mountains. Crematorium memorial building. Small museum in an old building (new Visitors Center is planned). Not much left that resembles a camp.

Former Main Gate, now a private residence

Crematorium Memorial

Air ventilation shaft from the tunnels built to hide underground munitions factories

Camp Opened: Dec 1939
Date Liberated: May 5, 1945

139

Schloss (Castle) Hartheim

Address: Verein Schloss Hartheim
Schlosstrasse 1
A-4072 Alkoven
Austria

Phone: 43+ 664 101 3730

E-mail: office@schloss-hartheim.at
Webpage: www.schloss-hartheim.at
www.nizkor.org/hweb/camps/gusen/gugas01x.htm

Hours: Daily 9am-6pm (check Website for current hours)

Entrance: Free (small fee for a "Guided" Tour)

Schedule: Plan on about 2 hours to see this site.

Location: About 12 miles west of Linz in Alkoven, Austria

Approx Train Travel Time to Alkoven:
From: Linz   .30
Mauthausen   2:00

By Train: From Linz you can get a train to Alkoven from the
Linz Lokalbahn station. This is a small local train
station a short walk from the Linz Hbf.

To reach Linz Lokalbahn station from Linz Hbf
(10 minute walk) Exit Linz Hbf and walk straight
ahead to the main street which is Kärntnerstrasse.
Cross over Kärntnerstrasse and turn Right.
You will come to the first intersection on the left,
where it forks: to the Left is Coulinstrasse & to the
Right is Volksgartenstrasse.
Go Left down Coulinstrasse for a short distance to
the Lokalbahn Station on the Left.

NOTE: Due to improvements at the Linz Hbf, the train to Alkoven may
eventually someday depart from *there* instead of the small
Lokalbahn station.

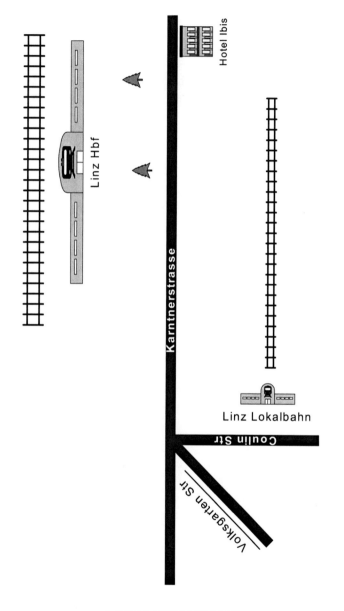

LINZ LOKALBAHN

To Walk: **10 Minutes** from the Alkoven Lokalbahn Station. Schloss Hartheim can be seen from Alkoven station. Exit the train and turn Right. Walk to the corner, near the 2 grain towers, turn Right and cross over the tracks. Look ahead and slightly to the right and you'll see the Spires of the Castle in the distance. This road is Dorfstrasse. Continue straight ahead and follow the road as it curves toward the castle. Turn Left on to Schlosstrasse. Enter through an opening in the wall surrounding the courtyard. This is the parking area.

By Car: Motorway A1 "West-Autobahn" to Wels (road B 134 or 137 to Eferding) or Linz (B 129 starts in Linz at the south-side bridge of the Danube), brown signs show the way to "Landesausstellung Schloss Hartheim" on the road B 129. Access is also possible from Passau (Passovie) on Road B 129.

Date Opened: 1938
Date Dismantled: 1944

Background: Like Hadamar (see Germany)
Schloss (Castle) Hartheim (a sixteenth Century Renaissance castle in Alkoven) was used to murder more of what the Nazis referred to as Useless Eaters. The mentally ill, retarded, handicapped or anyone deemed unfit by the Nazis where brought here and murdered.
Also sent here to be gassed were many prisoners of Mauthausen, Gusen and Dachau.
As was the case with some of the installations at the concentration camps, the Nazis dismantled the killing apparatus to try and cover up what they had been doing. Today, one can only try to visualize what it was like during operation.

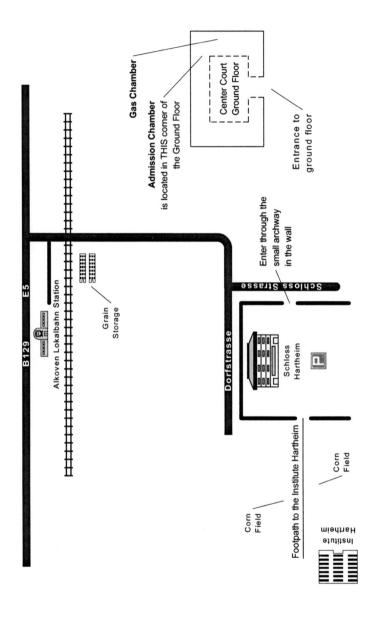

SCHLOSS HARTHEIM

143

What Remains:
In recent years this building has gone through a major renovation.
It is now a memorial museum dedicated to showing what took place
there. They have an exhibition called "Value of Life".
Visitors can walk through the various rooms and see documentation
(in German and English). The gas chamber is viewed from an elevated
bridge keeping visitors purposely at a distance.

Schloss (Castle) Hartheim

**Admission
Chamber**
area where victims
were undressed
and led to the
gas chamber

Ebensee

Address: KZ-Gedenkstätte und Zeitgeschichte Museum Ebensee
Kirchengasse 5
A-4802 Ebensee
Austria

Phone: +43 6133 5601
Fax: +43 6133 5601 4

E-mail: museum@utanet.at
Webpage: www.ebensee.org
http://motlc.wiesenthal.org/pages/t020/t02004.html

Hours: Cemetery open anytime.
The Tunnels are only open:
May, June, Oct.   on Sat. & Sun. 10am-5pm
July-Aug-Sept.   Tues. thru Sun. 10am-5pm
CLOSED MONDAYS

Entrance: Small Fee to enter the tunnel.

Schedule: Plan on about 15 minutes to view the cemetery
and about 30 minutes to see the tunnels (longer if
you are fortunate enough to be there when there is
a guide explaining the site).

Location: East of Salzburg, southwest of Linz.

Approx Train Travel Time to Ebensee Bahnhof
(not Ebensee Landungsplatz):

From:		
Linz	1:15
Mauthausen	2:16
Salzburg	1:37
Vienna (Wien)	3:22
Munich (München)	3:31

145

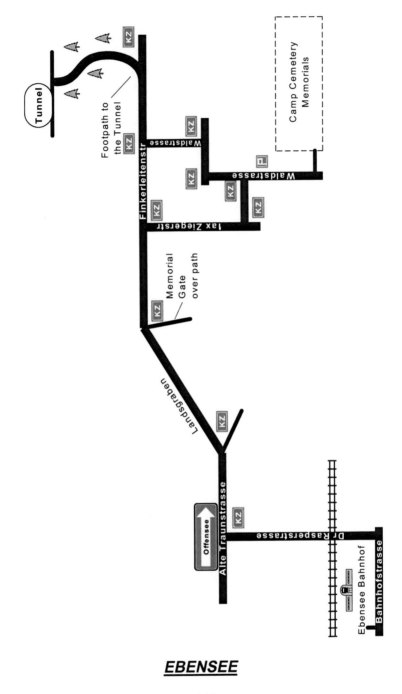

EBENSEE

146

To Walk:

1 Hour. From Ebensee Bahnhof (be sure you exit at THIS station and not Ebensee Landungsplatz which is another train station in this town). Exit Ebensee Bahnhof and walk ahead and slightly to the Right for a few steps until you get to the main street Bahnhofstrasse. Turn Left on Bahnhofstrasse and walk a few minutes until you can make a Left on "Dr. Rasperstrasse" which crosses over the railroad tracks and heads toward the mountains in the distance.

Go all the way down to the end (about 15 minutes) until you reach Alte Traunstrasse (which is NOT marked at the corner, but it is the end of Dr Rasperstrasse and where you can only go Left or Right. There is a sign that says "Offensee" at the intersection and a sign "KZ Ebensee" on the Right hand corner.

Turn Right and walk down until you come to a fork in the road (with a sign in the middle) where you go to the Left down Landsgraben. Continue down Landsgraben, you will pass a side street to the Right that has a memorial gate over the street

(do NOT turn here) keep going straight, the street becomes Finkerleitenstrasse. When you reach the corner of Finkerleitenstrasse and Max Ziegerstrasse you have a choice. The signs direct you to go to the Right down Max Ziegerstrasse through a residential neighbor-

hood. This leads directly to the small cemetery area. It is Well marked at Every Corner so you cannot get lost. BUT, if you wish to go Directly to the Tunnels, continue down Finkerleitenstrasse instead of turning and a short distance down on the Left will be a sign directing you along a path through the woods to the tunnel entrance. If you go to the cemetery first, signs will direct you from there along a different route to the tunnels.

(See the map for all the street names and routing)

Signs to the Cemetery say: KZ Gedenkstätte
Signs to the Tunnels say: KZ Gedenkstollen

By Car: From Bad Ischl or Gmunden on highway B145, take the exit Rindbach & follow the brown signs saying "KZ-Gedenkstätte". There are parking spaces in front of the cemetery. From there you can reach the exhibition in 3 minutes.

What Remains:

Nothing that resembles a concentration camp.
Small memorial cemetery with monuments and markers.
Tunnel built in the mountain by prisoners to build armaments.
A few descriptive signs inside with translations in English.

KZ Gedenkstollen
Sign leads the way to the tunnel

Entrance to the Tunnels at Ebensee.
Wear a coat, the temperature drops significantly inside.

CZECH REPUBLIC

Theresienstadt (Terezin)

Address:
(Admin. Offices)

Terezin Memorial
Principova alej 304
411 55 Terezin
Czech Republic

Phone: 420+ 416 - 782-225
Fax: 420+ 416 - 782-300

E-Mail: pamatnik@pamatnik-terezin.cz
Webpage(s): www.pamatnik-terezin.cz
www.cympm.com/teresin.html

Hours: Open Daily (see times Below)

Small Fortress: Oct 1 - March 31   8:00-4:30pm
April 1 – Sept 30   8:00-6:00pm

Ghetto Museum: Oct 1 - March 31   9:00-5:30pm
May 1 - Sept 30   9:00-6:00pm

Crematorium: Apr. 1 - Nov. 30 Daily (except Sat.) 10-5

Entrance: Small Fee. You can buy a ticket for the Fortress only, or (recommended) a ticket that gives you entrance to all exhibits.

Schedule: Plan on about 4 hours to visit both the Small Fortress, the Muzeum Ghetta and walking around to the Crematorium.

Location: Theresienstadt (Terezin) is about 40 miles (64½ km) north of Prague (Praha)

Guide Service is available in
English, German, Italian, Russian, Czech & French.

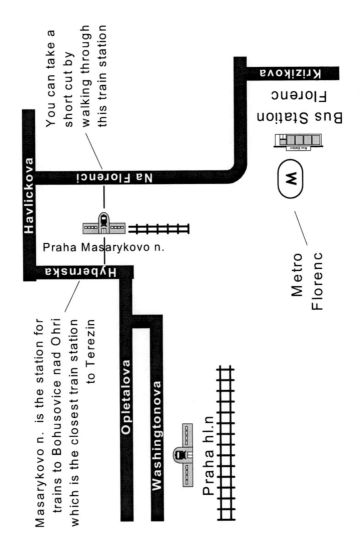

You can take a short cut by walking through this train station

Havlickova

Na Florenci

Praha Masarykovo n.

Hybernska

Masarykovo n. is the station for trains to Bohusovice nad Ohri which is the closest train station to Terezin

Opletalova

Washingtonova

Praha hl.n

Bus Station Florenc

Krizikova

Metro Florenc

W

PRAHA hl.n & FLORENC

Approx Train Travel Time to Prague (Praha hl.n):

From:
Berlin	5:23
Amsterdam	13:00
Krakow	12:54
Munich (München)	8:30
Linz	6:13

Prague/Public Transport:

www.odyssey.on.ca/~europrail/prague.htm

By Bus: Praha Florenc Bus station is about a 10 minute walk from Praha hl.n main train station or take the Metro.

To reach **Bus Station Florenc** from **Praha hl.n** train station you can take the Metro (**Line C**) located downstairs at the train station. Buy your Metro ticket from the Booths next to the stairs or from machines.

*You **MUST** validate your ticket by punching it in one of the Yellow Boxes located near the stairs or on the Metro.*

The Florence Metro station is only ONE stop north of the train station. From Florenc Metro station go up to street level and just a few steps behind the building next to the stairs is Bus Station Florenc.

You may pay the Bus driver, they make change. Buses make the 1 hour journey and drop you off right at the Mala Pevnost (Small Fortress) first and then you can walk to see the Ghetta Muzeum and Crematorium last. As always, write down your destination "Terezin Mala Pevnost" and show the driver as you board. Or you may pass the Small Fortress and do it in reverse.

If returning to Praha from the Muzeum Ghetta, the bus stop you want is at the corner of **Komenskeho & Namesti Cesklovenske Armady** (To the Right as you exit the Muzeum Ghetta building) It is **CSAD Bus Stop #1.** You will be going to Praha Florenc Bus Station.

```
┌─────────────────────────────────────────────┐
│              BUS SCHEDULE:                    │
│        Praha Florenc Station to Terezin       │
│  7:00, 9:00, 10:00, 11:00, 12:00, 13:00, 14:15│
│                                               │
│        Terezin to Praha Florenc Station       │
│  9:40, 12:55, 14:30, 15:35, 15:55, 18:10, 18:40│
└─────────────────────────────────────────────┘
```

By Train: NOT RECOMMENDED
1 Hour Walk after taking the train!

The nearest train station to Theresienstadt
(Terezin) is <u>Bohusovice nad Ohri</u>
(on the Prague-Dresden line).
To reach this station from Praha (Prague) you
should take the train from **Praha Masarykovo n.**
station (not **Praha hl.n** which is the main station)
Praha Masarykovo n. is located a few short
blocks from the main station (**Praha hl.n**) and can
be reached by foot in about 4 minutes.
Exit the Front of Praha hl.n station and turn Right.
Walk down to the first corner and turn Left. At the
Next corner you turn Right and straight ahead is
Praha Masarykovo n. station. This train takes 1
hour & 13 minutes to reach Bohusovice nad Ohri
Station. From there it is over a one hour walk.

To Walk: **1 Hour.** From Bohusovice nad Ohri station, exit
the station and turn Left. You will be on Nadrazni
Ulice. At the corner turn Right down Masarykova.
From here continue Straight ahead for about 30
minutes. The roads are Not marked, there are No
Signs mentioning Terezin or the Museum.
You will reach a fork in the road with a Green
Metal Fence. Keep to the Left and continue.

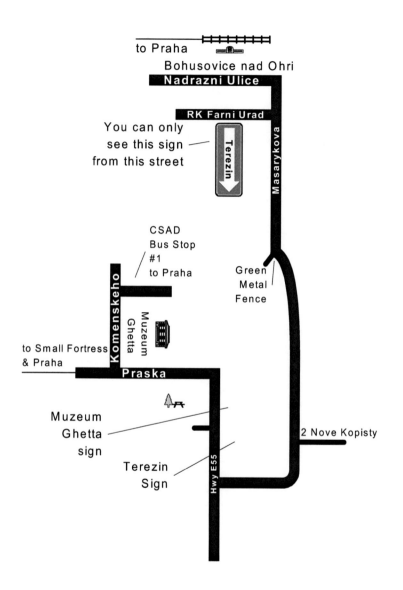

BOHUSOVICE nad OHRI STATION

You pass a road sign that says "2 Nove Kopisty" but continue forward. You finally reach a Major intersection which is Route **E55**. Turn Right and after a short walk you will see a sign "Terezin". Keep walking and you will pass a Park on the Left and the Muzeum Ghetta sign on the right. At the next corner turn Left down **Prazska**. The next corner is Machova and on the Right corner is the Muzeum Ghetta building. Continue down Prazska to the next corner which is **Komenskeho** and turn Right and there is the entrance to the Muzeum Ghetta.

Directions: If you took the bus and stopped first at the Mala Pevnost (Small Fortress) it's a 15 minute walk to the Muzeum Ghetta.

From the Small Fortress walk out to the road (main highway to Praha) and turn Right. Walk past the parking area, across the Bridge over the River Ohre keeping to the Right where you will continue down Prazska to Komenskeho where the Muzeum Ghetta building is located on the corner. After visiting the Museum, continue on to the Crematorium area.

<u>From the Muzeum Ghetta to the Crematorium/Cemetery
is a 15 minute walk.</u>
Exit the museum and turn Left. At the corner "Prazska" turn Left. Walk several blocks until you reach "Dlouha" and turn Left. Continue down this street (there is a sign along the way) until you reach the crematorium and cemetery area which will be off to the Left past the parking area (see signs).

What Remains:

Since Theresienstadt was a walled-in Ghetto similar to the Warsaw Ghetto it is difficult to explain what remains today.
Residential and Commercial property now sits on the former site.
There are many original buildings left, but few open to visitors.

The Mala Pevnost (Small Fortress) is enormous and a Must See.
Arbeit Macht Frei entrance, tunnels, exhibits and many buildings to walk through.

At the Muzeum Ghetta are many exhibits (also in English) and an excellent film (see front desk for English viewing time).

Crematorium Ovens

Medical Experimentation Room

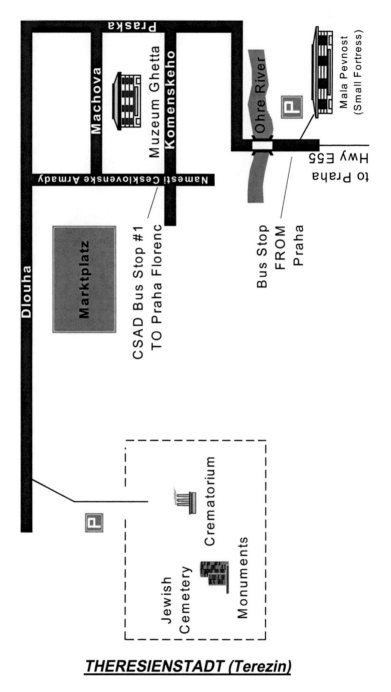

THERESIENSTADT (Terezin)

NOTE: They have an English brochure with a map and also on the back of the Entrance Ticket there is a map, BUT, this is very hard to figure out. The one on the back of the ticket has No Street Names and the one on the brochure shows street names, but they do not match the street signs! (therefore follow the map on previous page)

Recommended:
Unless you are very familiar with this area and the history of this place I suggest taking a guided tour. As with the Warsaw Ghetto, you can walk around on your own with a guide book but you won't get the full scope of what you are seeing. It will look like any other old city with homes, apartments, businesses etc.

**Cemetery at the entrance to the
Mala Pevnost (Small Fortress)**

Date Opened: June 1940 a police prison was established in the small fortress. November 1941 the ghetto camp was opened in the town.

Date Liberated: May 8, 1945

THE NETHERLANDS

AMSTERDAM Area

Approx Train Travel Time to Amsterdam CS (Centraal Station)

From:
Rotterdam CS	1:02
Berlin Zoolg. Garten	7:03
Munich (München)	10:34
Krakow Glowny	18:53
Brussels (Bruxelles Noord)	2:47

Amsterdam/Public Transport:
www.apti.is.nl
www.apti.is.nl/amsterdam.html

Amsterdam Centraal Station

Amsterdam is a great place to start your European travel.
Holland is a friendly, open-minded country where you'll find the majority of people speak English.
When you think of World War II, the Nazis & Concentration Camps you most likely wouldn't think of this country.
But there were several concentration camps on Dutch soil.
They were not the notorious Extermination Camps such as those in Poland, but they were horrible places none-the-less.

Anne Frank Huis (House)

Address: Prinsengracht 263
1016 GV Amsterdam, The Netherlands

or write:

ANNE FRANK STICHTING (Foundation)
PO Box 730
1000 AS Amsterdam
The Netherlands

Phone: 31+ 20 556 7100
Fax: 31+ 20 620 7999

E-mail: None Available
Webpage(s):
www.annefrank.nl
www.msnbc.com/onair/nbc/dateline/miepgies/annex.asp

Hours: Open Daily (See Website for Holiday Hours)
Apr. 1 – Aug. 31,   9am-9pm
Sept 1 – March 31, 9am-7pm

Entrance: Euro 6,50 (approx $7 US)

Schedule: Plan on about an hour to visit the house, longer
if you stay for the videos. Also plan on at least
a half hour wait in line to get in most times.

Location: Amsterdam not far from the Centraal Station

To Walk: Easily reached by foot, approximately 15 minute
walk from Centraal Train Station or 5 minutes
from Dam Square (the main square right in the
middle of shopping, restaurants, etc).
Exit the front of the Centraal Train Station walk
straight ahead across the bridge over the canal.
You will be walking down the Damrak (the main
street) which leads right to Dam Square.

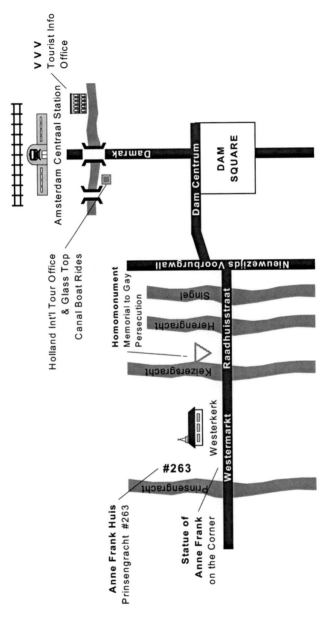

ANNE FRANK HUIS (House)

Once you reach the square (about 5 minute walk) immediately turn right down Dam Centrum. Walk down to the stop light, cross the street and you will be facing a building. Turn Left and walk a few steps and go Right down Raadhuisstraat. Cross over 3 canals: Singel, Herengracht & Keizersgracht. (Notice the Triangular Monument jutting out into the Keizersgracht canal). This is the "**Homomonument**" dedicated to those who have been persecuted for being Gay.

The 4th canal you come to is Prinsengracht and on the Corner is the Westerkerk (West Church). Turn Right at the Church (statue of Anne Frank is located at the front Left Corner of the Church as you turn the corner). Walk down Prinsengracht about a half block past the Church to the house at **Prinsengracht 263**.

The front of the original entrance at 263 is painted dark green. A new wing of the museum opened in the Fall of 1999 and you now enter through a modern area to the Right of the original house at #267. You can't miss it, or the lines waiting to get in. The Anne Frank Huis (House) is the Most Visited site in Amsterdam.

Original House Entrance Above Left.   New Entrance on the Right.

Another view of the original house #263 on the Left, and the lines at the new entrance on the Right.

GET THERE EARLY!
I visit Amsterdam often & have been to the Anne Frank House many times. Years ago you could arrive anytime of the day and walk right in. Now, since Schindler's List and all the interest in the Holocaust, the lines can be VERY long. It's an experience worth the wait!

Recommended Viewing: **The Diary of Anne Frank (1959)**
B/W 156 min.
Millie Perkins as Anne Frank
Available on Video.

Anne Frank Remembered (1995)
Color 117 min.
Available on Video.
Columbia TriStar Home Video

(Shown on a monitor at the House)

Recommended Reading: **The Diary of a Young Girl -**
ANNE FRANK
Edited by Otto H. Frank
and Mirjam Pressler
Bantam Books

Anne Frank Remembered
The Story of the Woman Who
Helped Hide the Frank Family
Miep Gies with Alison Leslie Gold
1987 Touchstone Books.
Published by Simon & Schuster

Date Family Went into Hiding: Monday, 6 July, 1942

Date They Were Arrested: Friday, 4 August 1944
(around Noon)

What Remains:

It's very small and cramped upstairs. You walk up VERY STEEP (Ladder-Like) stairs, through the Bookcase that covered the hiding place and into the rooms. You see Anne's movie star pictures on the wall along with her diary which is there in a glass case.
It's Very Moving and Emotional. Bring Tissues! Stay for the video if you can. No Pictures or Videotaping is allowed, but they have a gift shop at the exit which has some very good books with lots of excellent pictures & information.

Actress Shelley Winters won a Supporting Actress Academy Award for her role as Mrs. Van Daan in the 1959 movie version of The Diary of Anne Frank. She donated her Oscar to the house and it is sometimes on display there.

The Bookcase that hid the entrance to the attic hiding place.

Today, visitors can walk behind the bookcase and visit the rooms where the 8 people hid for 2 years before being arrested.

163

Ravensbrück Memorial

Address: Monument on Museumplein in Amsterdam

Website: http://home.wxs.nl/~jvansant/rav.html

By Tram:
Take Circle Tram #20 (see Amsterdam/Public Transport)
from the Centraal Station to the Rijksmuseum.
3 Guilders (you may pay the conductor at the back, they make
change) or buy a Stripkarten (one charge for all day). Stamp it each
time you get on. (fold over before stamping each time). Good until it
is used up. If you are traveling longer distances you may need to
stamp it more than once for different zones, but for the Rijksmuseum, stamp it once. Exit the tram at the Rijksmuseum and turn Left.
You'll be on Hobbemastraat. About 30 feet is the corner of Paulus
Potter Straat. Turn Right and then make a Left at the next corner
Honthorstraat (Vincent statue on the left corner). Passing a grassy
park area on the right you come to Museumplein where you turn
Right. The Ravensbrück Monument is a few steps to your Right.
Pick up the Tram BACK at the same spot you arrived.
It makes a Circle back to Centraal Station.

Monument: A Large Steel Column Structure.
This is the memorial to the Women of Ravensbrück Concentration
Camp (in Fürstenberg, North of Berlin).

Those women
(among them
Corrie Ten Boom
and her sister
Betsie) resisted the
Nazis and helped
save lives during
the war.
There is nothing
to see here except
the Steel Columns,

but if you are visiting the Rijksmuseum and are interested, it will
only take you about 5 minutes to walk back to see this and perhaps
take a photo.

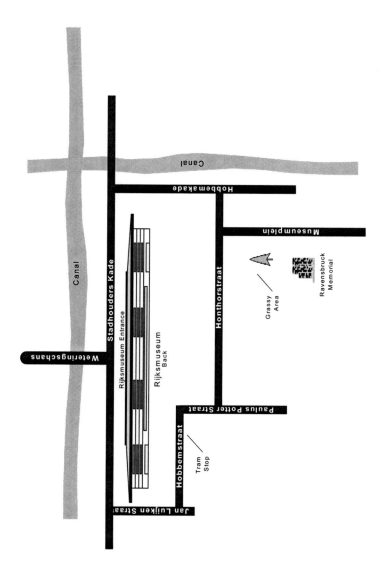

RAVENSBRÜCK MEMORIAL

Corrie Ten Boom House *"The Hiding Place"*

Address: Barteljorisstraat 19
2011 RA Haarlem, Holland

Phone: 31+23-5310823
Fax: 31+23-5251515

E-mail: None Available
WebSite(s):   www.corrietenboom.com
www.soon.org.uk/true_stories/holocaust.htm

Hours: April 1 to October 31
    Open Tuesday-Saturday 10am-4pm.
November 1 to March 31
    Open Tuesday-Saturday 11am-3pm.
CLOSED SUNDAY & MONDAY
and some days for holidays.

Entrance: Free

Schedule: Plan on about 1 hour for the Tour.

Location: Haarlem, Holland a short walk from the station.

Approx Train Travel Time to Haarlem:
From: Amsterdam   0:15
    Rotterdam   0:51

To Walk: Exit Haarlem station (Centrum exit) and turn
Right. At the end of that street on the Right Side is
the familiar **VVV** Tourist Information Office.
(**VVV** offices are located throughout Holland and
are very helpful with free information on everything, including helping with hotel reservations if
needed). Bus stops are at this corner also.
That street at the end is called Kruisweg.
Turn LEFT. Walk down Kruisweg
(Kruisweg changes names to Kruisstraat).
Walk straight down this street crossing several
canals until you come to a fork in the road where it
splits 3 ways.

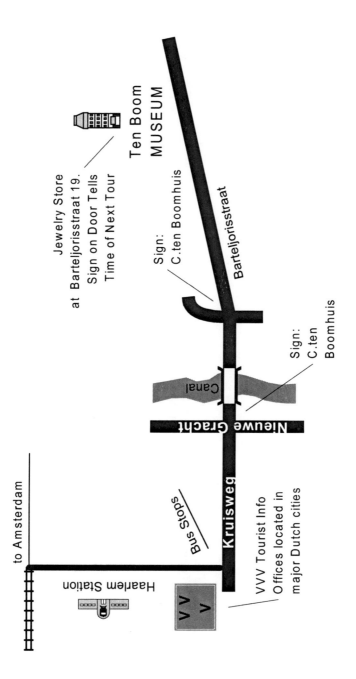

Jewelry Store
at Barteljorisstraat 19.
Sign on Door Tells
Time of Next Tour

Ten Boom
MUSEUM

Barteljorisstraat

Sign:
C.ten Boomhuis

Sign:
C.ten
Boomhuis

Canal

Nieuwe Gracht

to Amsterdam

Bus Stops

Kruisweg

VVV Tourist Info
Offices located in
major Dutch cities

Haarlem Station

CORRIE TEN BOOM HOUSE

C ten Boomhuis

These signs lead the way to the museum

Stay in the middle and the street becomes Barteljorisstraat (a store lined street).
Look for Number 19 (a Jewelry Store) on the Left Side.
A Red & White Clock & Sign says **"Ten Boom MUSEUM"** Can't Miss It!

What Remains:
Guided Tours Only.
Upstairs are the rooms of the Family Ten Boom. The Hiding Place in Corrie's room, many pictures & documents telling the story. The tour consists of telling the story of what happened in the house and also concentrates on Corrie's strong religious faith. The Tour lasts approximately 1 hour.
It is Free of charge although they do ask for a voluntary donation in their blessing box.

Tours in English usually begin around 10am.
There is a sign on the door that tells the time of the next tour.
Wait Outside, the guide will come out to greet you at the given time.
You may take pictures and some video if you like
(unlike the Anne Frank House where photography is not permitted.

Year They Started Hiding People: 1942
Date They Were Arrested: February 28, 1944

Background: Corrie and her sister were caught and sent to Ravensbrück camp. Betsie died of illness and Corrie was released (in error) shortly before all women her age were executed. It's an amazing story. If you have a chance to see the 1975 Film with Julie Harris (The Hiding Place) or read the book, I'd do it before you go. Likewise with the Diary of Anne Frank, it makes it much more meaningful.

NOTE: Corrie Ten Boom died on her 91st birthday (April 15, 1983) and is buried in Fairhaven Memorial Park in Santa Ana, California (So.California/Orange County/Los Angeles area) 1702 East Fairhaven Ave., Santa Ana, California (714) 633-1442. *LAWN A, LOT 501, SP A*

Recommended Viewing: **The Hiding Place (1975)**
Color 147 min.
Julie Harris as Betsie Ten Boom
Available on Video
Republic Pictures

Recommended Reading: The Hiding Place
By Corrie Ten Boom
with John & Elizabeth Sherrill
Spire Books

The Hiding Place

The people had to climb into the small opening at the bottom of the linen closet.

Today, visitors can see the tiny space inside where they hid when the police came to arrest Corrie and her family.

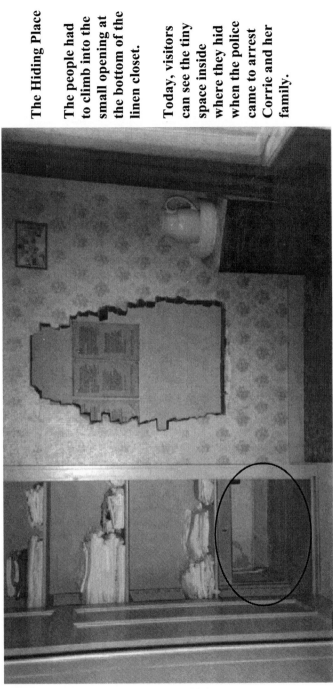

Westerbork

Address: Herinneringscentrum (Commemoration Centre)
Kamp Westerbork
Oosthalen 8
9414 TG Hooghalen
The Netherlands

Phone: 31+ 593 592600
Fax: 31+ 593 592546

Email: info@kampwesterbork.nl

Webpage(s): www.westerbork.nl
http://users.skynet.be/sky35373/westerbe.htm
www.cympm.com/Westerbork.html

Hours: Monday-Friday   10:00-5:00
Saturday/Sunday   1:00-5:00
(Sat-Sun in July and August   11:00-5:00)
Closed December 25 & 31 and January 1
(Check website for changes to opening times)

Entrance: Euro 3,85 (approx $4 US)

Schedule: Plan on about 2½ Hours to see this site.
Tell the Trein-Taxi Driver to reserve your ride
back in about 2 ½ hours (longer if you like to
closely study each exhibit) or Call the Assen
Trein-Taxi office 0592 37 3111

Location: Northern Netherlands between Assen & Beilen.

Approx Train Travel Time to Assen:
From:

Amsterdam	1:55
Vught	2:50
Amersfoort	1:20
Berlin	8:19

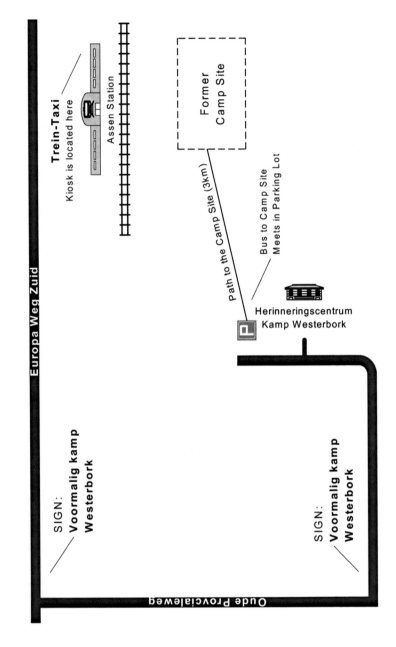

Europa Weg Zuid

Trein-Taxi
Kiosk is located here

Assen Station

Former Camp Site

Path to the Camp Site (3km)

Bus to Camp Site
Meets in Parking Lot

Herinneringscentrum
Kamp Westerbork

SIGN:
**Voormalig kamp
Westerbork**

SIGN:
**Voormalig kamp
Westerbork**

Oude Provcialeweg

<u>WESTERBORK</u>

By Train: From Amsterdam take a train to Assen (northeast of Amsterdam).

Trein-Taxi: Exit the front of the Assen train station and turn Right. Look for the Blue/Yellow Trein-Taxi (Train-Taxi) Kiosk. Take the Trein-Taxi to Herinneringscentrum Kamp Westerbork in the Village of Hooghalen (approx 10 minutes) Although most people in Holland speak English, I suggest writing down where you are going: **"Herinneringscentrum Kamp Westerbork"** to show the driver when they ask your destination.

Yellow Ticket Machines are Marked
(Trein Kaartjes)
The machines are very easy to use.
On the Top Row of options look for "Trein-Taxi"
#1 Punch in the Number for Trein-Taxi
   (ie: 0757)
#2 Display will show amount to insert
#3 Deposit Coins
#4 Take Ticket

Bus from the Museum to the Campsite:

After visiting the museum, take the bus (small fee for Roundtrip ticket) to the camp site. Pay the driver, they make change. The bus stop is located in the Car Park area and leaves several times an hour. You CAN walk or take a bike there, it's approximately 2.2 km (1½ miles) from the car park area and is clearly marked.

TREIN-TAXI
You do NOT need to have a Train Ticket to use the Trein-Taxi.

Trein-Taxi (train-taxi) stops are located
at most major rail stations in Holland.

THIS IS HOW IT WORKS:
Buy a Trein-Taxi ticket in the
station (either at the domestic
ticket windows "Binnenland" or
the yellow automated machines)
NOTE:
If you don't buy a ticket Beforehand, you CAN buy one from
the Taxi Driver (they make
change) but it will cost a couple
dollars more:
Tipping the Driver is apparently
not expected, (I didn't see anyone doing it) but I gave them a
small tip because I asked a lot of
questions and they were very
helpful. It's up to you.

When you arrive at the Trein-
Taxi Kiosk you queue up with
others waiting for a ride. The
driver will ask each person
where they are going. (They
usually fill the cab with all the
people going in the same general
direction) You might be the first stop, or you might be the last stop,
or they might ask you to wait for the next taxi because the majority
of those standing in line are going in the opposite direction)
When you get to your destination you have *Two Choices*, you CAN
Reserve the Return Journey with the Driver by telling them to pick
you up at a certain time, OR, you can call the Trein-Taxi phone
number for that town (ask the driver for it if you don't have a Trein-
Taxi guide) when you are ready to leave and they will come and
pick you up. I suggest reserving with the driver (saves trying to find
a payphone etc). I've noted approximately how much time you
should need to see each site.

By Car: Take the A28 Motorway to Beilen or Assen-Zuid. Turn off for Hooghalen and follow the signs to **"Voormalig kamp Westerbork"**

(Do NOT go to the Village of Westerbork)

What Remains:

At the Museum:
Exhibits (mostly in Dutch).
Ask for the English guidebook
to use (& return) while you walk
through the museum.
Cinema (film showing the
history of Westerbork)
Books/Videos for Sale.

At the Campsite:
Very little of the original camp remains.
There are a few *reconstructed* facades of buildings, some memorial markers, guard tower, and train track monument.
Unrelated to the camp are huge Radio Transmitter Dishes located in the vicinity of the grounds.

Original sign from the side of one of the transport trains that took prisoners from Westerbork to Auschwitz and returned for more.

Background:

Westerbork was a "Transit" Camp. Prisoners were sent here to await being sent to concentration camps in the East such as Auschwitz and Sobibór. Among those who spent time in Westerbork were Anne Frank and her family. The prisoners were given a sense of "False Hope" while they stayed here. They were allowed to have Talent Shows and put on plays and skits. They sent letters home telling how things weren't so bad here. Then every Tuesday a train would pull in and those selected the night before would be sent to the extermination camps in the East. Right up until they arrived at places such as Auschwitz or Sobibór they still thought things were going to be ok.

93 Transports left Westerbork, usually for Auschwitz or Sobibór.

Approximately 107,000 Jews & 245 Gypsies were shipped from here.

Reconstructed facade of the barracks where Anne Frank & family spent their last days before being shipped to the camps

Memorial Markers for the countless thousands who were transported from Westerbork to their deaths at camps in the East such as Sobibór and Auschwitz.

Less than 5000 Survived and returned after the war.

Camp Opened:

In 1939 as a Camp for Jewish Refugees from Germany. In 1942 it became a Transit Camp to ship Jews to the East.

Date Liberated:

April 12, 1945 by Canadian forces.

Vught

Address: National Monument Camp Vught
Lunettenlaan 600

Mailing Address: Stichting Nationaal Monument Kamp Vught
Postbus 47
5260 AA Vught
The Netherlands

Phone: 31+73 656 6764
Fax: 31+73 658 7068

E-Mail: info@nmkampvught.nl

Webpage: www.nmkampvught.nl
www.cympm.com/vught.html

Hours: January 20 to December 19
Tuesday-Friday 10am-5pm
Saturday-Sunday Noon-5pm
CLOSED MONDAYS

Entrance: Free

Schedule: Plan on about 1½ hours to see this sight and walk
to the firing range.
If just visiting the museum, 1 hour is plenty.

Location: Southeast of Amsterdam, Holland

Approx Train Travel Time to Vught:
From:

Amsterdam	1:18
Assen	2:50
Amersfoort	0:57
Brussels (Bruxelles Noord)	2:36
Berlin	7:41

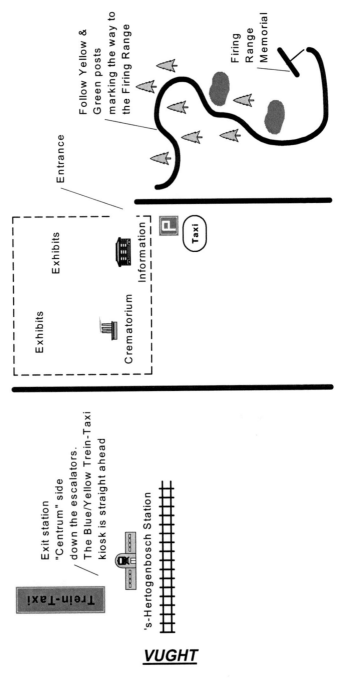

Follow Yellow &
Green posts
marking the way to
the Firing Range

Firing
Range
Memorial

Entrance

Exhibits

Exhibits

Crematorium

Information

Taxi

Exit station
"Centrum" side
down the escalators.
The Blue/Yellow Trein-Taxi
kiosk is straight ahead

Trein-Taxi

's-Hertogenbosch Station

VUGHT

178

By Train:

To a station called **'s-Hertogenbosch.** From Amsterdam take the Intercity train in the direction of Eindhoven, Maastricht which runs several times each hour in both directions. Exit at ' s-Hertogenbosch and then take the "Trein-Taxi" (see WESTERBORK) from there directly to the memorial. Exit ' s-Hertogenbosch station, go downstairs to the street "Centrum exit" The blue/yellow Trein-Taxi kiosk is straight ahead as you come down the escalator. Write down where you want to go **"Monument Kamp Vught"** to show the driver. Tell the driver to be back in 1½ hours to pick you up.

By Car:

Amsterdam – Utrecht take the A2 South to ' s-Hertogenbosch. Then go 10-15 minutes toward Tilburg then 3 traffic lights following the signs to **Nationaal Monument Kamp Vught.**

What Remains:

Visitors center with exhibits in Dutch. A small cinema, crematorium, dissection room and a reconstructed prisoners barrack. English brochures or an English tour guide can be arranged for a minimal charge.

Entrance to the Memorial at Vught

There is a firing range memorial in the woods (see Map)
(approximately a 10 minute walk from the main museum).
Take the paths located outside the entrance near the parking area.

Follow these green and yellow
posts with Vught symbol along the
trail to get there.
(see picture on back cover)

Symbol of Vught Camp

Memorial at the Firing Range

Camp Opened: January 1943
Date Liberated: September 1944

Amersfoort

Address: Gedenkplaats Kamp Amersfoort
Appelweg 1
3832 RK Leusden

Phone: 31+33 462 8000

E-Mail: info@kampamersfoort.nl
Webpage(s): www.kampamersfoort.nl
www.cympm.com/amersfoort.html

Hours: Monday-Friday 8:00am-6:00pm
Closed Saturdays-Sundays and some holidays
(Check Website for Current opening hours)

Entrance: Free

Schedule: Plan on about 30 minutes to see this site

Location: Southeast of Amsterdam, Holland.

Approx Train Travel Time to Amersfoort:
From:

Amsterdam	0:39
Vught	0:57
Assen	1:19
Berlin	6:22

By Taxi: Take a Trein-Taxi from Amersfoort train station.

By Bus: Bus #4 will take you from the train station
to Balistraat (see map) from there it is only
a 10 minute walk.

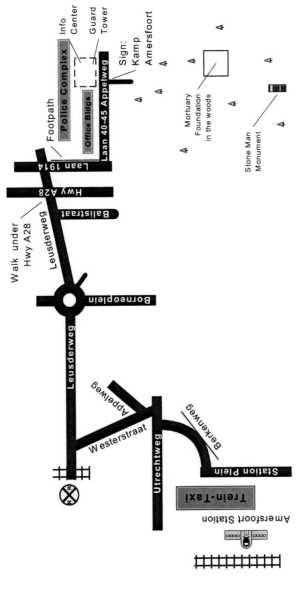

AMERSFOORT

182

To Walk:	<u>45 Minutes.</u>
Exit the front of Amersfoort station and cross the street and turn Left. Turn Right down Berkenweg (Azko building on the corner). Turn Right on Utrechtsweg and a few more blocks turn Left down Westerstraat which curves to the Left (crossing Appelweg). Turn Right down Leusderweg. Continue past Van Campen Straat. When you reach a Round-a-bout by Borneoplein go around and continue down Leusderweg passing Balistraat, going under the main highway A28 to the next corner of Laan 1914. Cross over and turn Right. Walk about 5 minutes down the footpath until you reach a corner with the sign **Verzetsmonument**, Laan 40-45 Appelweg and turn Left. About 5 minutes down that road is a small sign Kamp Amersfoort on the Right and the Guard tower behind a fence on the Left.

What Remains:

A guard tower and a small museum building showing a video. The site is located in what is now a police training complex across from a golf course. In the woods across the street are several partial foundations of buildings, and a few memorial statues but little more. Ask for an English brochure or print out the map from their website so you'll know what you can see in the woods and surrounding area.

183

FRANCE

Natzweiler-Struthof (Natzwiller)

Address: Direction Interdepartementale
des Anciens Combattants et Victimes
de Guerre Service de Strasbourg
Cite Administrative
67084 Strasbourg Cedex

Phone: 33+ 3+ 88 76 78 99
Fax: 33+ 3+ 88 76 78 89

E-mail: None Available
Webpage: www.us-israel.org/jsource/Holocaust/natztoc.html

Hours: 1 March to 30 June
10:00am-12noon, then 2:00pm-5:30pm
1 July to 31 August
10:00am-6:00pm (no interruption)
1 September to 24 December
10:00am-12noon, then 2:00pm-5:00pm

Entrance: Small fee
Tickets are NOT sold during the half hour before
the Noon closing and the hour before the Evening
closing.

Schedule: Plan on about 1 hour to visit this site

Location: Near the town of Natzwiller, 50km (31 miles)
south of Strasbourg on a hill in the Vosges
Mountains.

Approx Train Travel Time to Strasbourg:

From:
Berlin	10:38
Amsterdam	9:53
Krakow	17:54
Munich (München)	4:58
Paris	5:45

This camp is NOT easy to get to unless you have a car. There are NO buses from Rothau to the camp and I didn't notice any taxis near the station.

By Car: From Strasbourg travel Southwest to Rothau on the N420. Take a Left heading East on the D130 road in Rothau following the signs up the mountain to the camp entrance (8km–5mi) It is clearly marked "LE STRUTHOF" along the way.

You do NOT want to go to Natzwiller SEE MAP

By Train: From Strasbourg take a train to Rothau (1 hour) (No baggage lockers or storage at Rothau station)

To Walk: **2 Hours & 10 Minutes** from Rothau Station.
It's an UPHILL walk all the way
(No Restrooms!)
When you leave the train, the station will be on the left. Walk Behind the station and turn Right and walk to the corner and turn Left.
(Sign says D730 Rothau Center). At the next intersection (Route N420) you'll see signs on Both corners directing you to go straight ahead up the D130 to Natzwiller & Struthof.

185

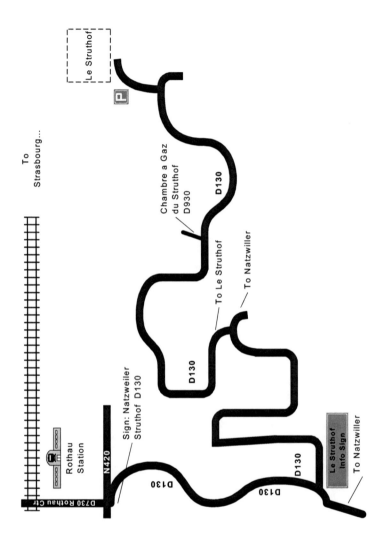

Le STRUTHOF

186

See MAP for details of the route. It's not a difficult walk (incline is gradual) but it's a **LONG** walk and there's not as much to see here as there is at some of the other camp memorials. You need to decide for yourself if it's worth the trek.

Recommend:
Rent a car, or take a Taxi (if you can find one at Rothau) or go on an organized Tour from Strasbourg.

What Remains:
Entrance Gate, barrack building with a few exhibits.

There is a HUGE impressive monument & cemetery.

Unless you are in the area and are set on going to this site for a certain reason, I wouldn't suggest making the journey. It's very difficult to reach, they charge you to get in, and what there is to see takes less than an hour.

A sign leads you to the gas chamber building on a side road before you get to the camp entrance (see MAP), but that isn't always open to the public.

Camp Opened:
May 1, 1941

Date Liberated:
September 1944

HELPFUL TRAVEL HINTS

24-HOUR CLOCK:
In Europe you'll need to get used to seeing schedules
listed in Military Time (24-Hour)

12:00 Noon	19:00 7pm	1:00 1am	7:00 7am
13:00 1pm	20:00 8pm	2:00 2am	8:00 8am
14:00 2pm	21:00 9pm	3:00 3am	9:00 9am
15:00 3pm	22:00 10pm	4:00 4am	10:00 10am
16:00 4pm	23:00 11pm	5:00 5am	11:00 11am
17:00 5pm	24:00 Midnight	6:00 6am	12:00 Noon
18:00 6pm			

TRAIN SCHEDULE POSTINGS:
In most train stations the schedules are posted on the walls.
YELLOW SCHEDULE is usually DEPARTURES
WHITE SCHEDULE is usually ARRIVALS
Many stations also have Electronic Boards announcing the
Departures and Arrivals for the next few hours.

TRAIN TIMETABLE WEBSITE:
This Website is Great for planning your rail trips BEFORE you go. It's
the Deutsche Bahn (German Rail), but has almost ALL the major
trains in Europe on it. You can see what time trains go, how many
stops and how long it will take.

http://reiseauskunft.bahn.de/bin/query.exe/en

EURAILPASS VALIDATION:
You **MUST** have your rail passes Validated **BEFORE** getting on your
first train trip. This can be done at ticket windows in the train station.
You need to show your passport and, very important, make sure they
write down the CORRECT START DATE & ENDING DATE.
In Europe dates are written: Day/Month/Year (ie: 5/12/99 for Dec 5)
It's best to write down the date you want to START your travel to
show them in case there is a language problem.

RAIL PASS WEBSITE:
Here is a great website address for checking on various pass options.

www.railpass.com

INFORMATION: In most cases look for a BIG **i**
They usually have someone who speaks English, but not always.

CHANGING MONEY:
In most airports and train stations there are banks/money changing
windows. The rate of exchange can vary from one to another so check
around to get the most for your money. If you are NOT going to be
changing large amounts, this is not as important. For the BEST rate it
is sometimes wise to use your ATM or Credit Card in machines and
then you'll get the bank rate without the added fee that independent
money change booths charge. (Check with YOUR bank to see what
fees they charge for international use). Money will be given in Local
Currency, so you'll need to figure out how much you want before
approaching the machines or the windows. If you are changing
Travelers Checks, be prepared to show your passport.
DO NOT...I REPEAT...do **NOT** change money with people who
approach you on the street or in the train stations.
They will say they can give you a better rate. Don't Trust Them!

MONEY BELTS/SAFETY:
Always carry the BULK of your money/travelers checks/airline
tickets & Passport in a Safe Place. A money belt worn under your shirt
works fine. I usually carry enough money for the day in my front pants
pocket. If traveling on trains, I keep my passport and train tickets/pass
handy to show the conductors.
Be aware of your surroundings, don't be paranoid, just careful.

ELECTRICITY/VOLTAGE ADAPTERS:
Europe has 220V. If you are taking along electrical appliances,
(hairdryers, video recharging devices etc) you will need to carry
along an adapter since the US is 110V. Conveniently, many small
travel hairdryers as well as some video charging stands are now
"Dual Voltage" so you don't need to take along a Voltage Adapter.
Some automatically switch to 220V when used in Europe, others
require you to manually select the 220V or 110V on the appliance.

PLUGS:
Unlike the Flat Prong Plug used in the States, all the countries
covered in this guide use a Round Prong Plug. (England uses 3-prong)
Voltage Adapter kits come with these plug attachments.

TOILETS/RESTROOMS (This can be a Trip by Itself!)
BE PREPARED! The "Pay Toilet" lives in Europe!
With few exceptions, plan on paying as you go. (no pun intended).
It's not much, normally the equivalent of a few cents US, so keep
Small Change in the *Local Currency* handy for this necessity.
In many places Restrooms are denoted by a sign that says **"WC"**
which stands for Water Closet. There will usually be a female
attendant sitting there guarding the entrance.

Here's the Drill:
Place your payment in the plate or dish she has sitting on the table at
the entrance (don't even THINK about sneaking in without paying).
In some WC's (not all) Men have a choice to make. If we are going to
only use the urinal (pissoir) it might be one price, if we need to
use the stall it's more. Check the sign, pay the correct amount.

The Plot Thickens:
On my last trip through Poland I noticed a new twist to pay toilets.
On the table, next to the plate where you put your change was a
Roll of Toilet Paper! I took a lucky guess that this meant there is
none in the stalls and that I needed to take enough off the roll before
I went in. (my guess was correct)

Just When You Think You've Seen It All:
At one restroom it must have been a slow day or something, but the
lady sitting there guarding the plate and toilet paper had torn off
all the separate single ply sheets and folded them neatly like little
napkins on the table. In THIS scenario you need to think quickly.
How many sheets do I need? 5?... 17? Do I take her whole supply?
Heaven forbid you should come up short sheeted and have to wave
over the stall for some more!

Women in the Men's Room:
Yes Gents, the lady guard and cleaners might show up in the mens
room doing their cleaning while you're in there doing your business.
This is normal, get over it…..When in Rome….yadda yadda yadda

Going on the Train:
Just in case you've ever wondered, Yes, when you flush, it DOES
go on the tracks! So, they frown on those using the WC while it is
IN the station. Go Before the Train Stops!

Free Toilets:
On the Train, in Most Airports, some Fast Food Restaurants.

TOUR GUIDES:

POLAND

East-West Guiding Agency owned by the Nowodworski family

Tel/Fax: 48 + 81 + 444 09 00
Email(s): superharp@inetia.pl
nowosan@poczta.onet.pl

Located in Lublin, Poland, this agency offers friendly, reliable service and reasonable rates on tours to many of the Holocaust sites including: Majdanek and former Nazi buildings as well as the ghetto in Lublin and many pre-war Jewish sites.

GERMAN CHARACTER ß

In Germany/Austria whenever you see the character ß it stands for a double "ss' (ie: Straße) which is Strasse or Street.

KZ and KL
Abbreviations for *Konzentrationslager* (Concentration Camp)

SS
Schutzstaffel or Protection Squad. Hitler's bodyguards who became the driving force behind the Death Camps.

HELPFUL WEBSITES:

U.S. HOLOCAUST MEMORIAL MUSEUM (Washington)
www.ushmm.org

WORLDWIDE SUBWAY PAGE
www.reed.edu/~reyn/transport.html

MUSEUM of TOLERANCE
www.wiesenthal.com/mot

YAD VASHEM in ISRAEL
www.yad-vashem.org.il

THE FORGOTTEN CAMPS
www.jewishgen.org/ForgottenCamps/index.html

A TEACHERS GUIDE TO THE HOLOCAUST
http://fcit.usf.edu/holocaust/RESOURCE/GALLERY/gallery5.htm

USEFUL WORDS YOU MIGHT NEED

POLISH

Airport	Lotnisko	Passport	Paszport
Arrival	Przyjazd	Platform	Peron
Baggage	Bagaz	Reservation	Rezerwowac
Bus	Autobus	Telephone	Telefon
Closed	Zamkniety	Thank-you	Dziekuje
Departure	Odjazd	Ticket	Bilet
Entrance	Wejscie	Toilet	Toaleta
Exit	Wyjscie	Track	Tor
Information	Informacja	Train	Pociag
Open	Otwarty		

GERMAN

Airport	Flughafen	Passport	Pass
Arrival	Ankunft	Platform	Bahnsteig
Baggage	Gepaeck	Reservation	Reservierungen
Bus	Autobus	Reserved	Reserviert
Closed	Geschlossen	Telephone	Telefon
Departure	Abfahrt	Thank-you	Danke
Entrance	Eingang	Ticket	Fahrkarte
Exit	Ausgang	Toilet	Toilette
Men	Herren	Track	Gleis
Money Change	Geldwechsel	Train	Zug
Open	Offen	Women	Damen

CZECH

Airport	Letiste	Open	Otevreno
Arrival	Prijezd	Passport	Pas
Baggage	Zavazadlo	Platform	Nabrezi
Bus	Autobus	Reserve	Uchovati
Closed	Zavreno	Telephone	Telefon
Departure	Odjezdy	Thank-you	Dekuji
Entrance	Vchod	Ticket	Jizdenka
Exit	Vychod	Toilet	Toaleta
Information	Informace	Train	Vlak

DUTCH

Airport	Luchthaven	Passport	Paspoort
Arrival	Aankomst	Platform	Perron
Baggage	Bagage	Reservation	Reservering
Bus	Bus	Reserved	Gereserveerd
Closed	Gesloten	SmokingRoken	
Departure	Vertrek	Telephone	Telefoon
Entrance	Ingang	Thank-you	Danku
Exit	Uitgang	Ticket	Kaartje
Information	Informatie	Toilet	Toilet
Men	Heren	Track	Spoor
Money	Geld	Train	Trein
Open	Openen	Women	Vrouw

In the Train Station

Binnenland	Ticket Counter for travel WITHIN Holland
Sneltrein	Fast Train (usually only stops at major stations)
Stoptrein	Stops at more of the smaller stations along the way

FRENCH

Airport	Aeroport	Open	Ouvert
Arrival	Arrivee	Passport	Passeport
Baggage	Bagages	Platform	Terrasse
Bus	Autobus	SmokingFumant	
Closed	Ferme	Telephone	Telephone
Departure	Depart	Thank-you	Merci
Entrance	Entrée	Ticket	Billet
Exit	Sortie	Toilet	Toilette
Information	Informations	Track	Voie
Lockers	Casier	Women	Dames
Men	Hommes		

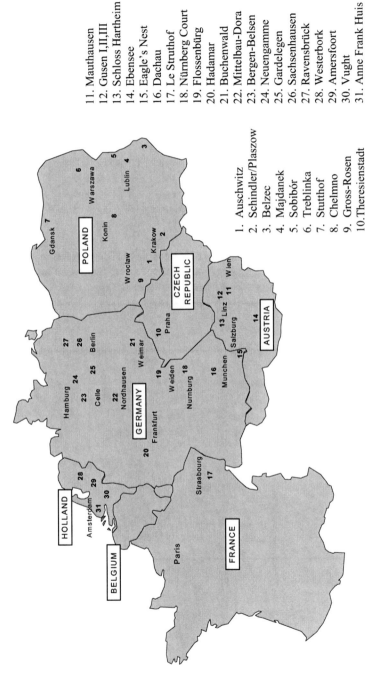

11. Mauthausen
12. Gusen I,II,III
13. Schloss Hartheim
14. Ebensee
15. Eagle's Nest
16. Dachau
17. Le Struthof
18. Nürnberg Court
19. Flossenbürg
20. Hadamar
21. Buchenwald
22. Mittelbau-Dora
23. Bergen-Belsen
24. Neuengamme
25. Gardelegen
26. Sachsenhausen
27. Ravensbrück
28. Westerbork
29. Amersfoort
30. Vught
31. Anne Frank Huis

1. Auschwitz
2. Schindler/Plaszow
3. Belzec
4. Majdanek
5. Sobibór
6. Treblinka
7. Stutthof
8. Chelmno
9. Gross-Rosen
10. Theresienstadt

INDEX